How To Teach Children
Twice As Much

How To Teach Children Twice As Much

ALLAN E. HARRISON

ARLINGTON HOUSE   NEW ROCHELLE, N.Y.

I dedicate this book to all
the children of the world.

Library of Congress Catalog Card Number: 73-11579

Manufactured in the United States of America

Library of Congress Cataloging in Publication Data

Harrison, Allan E
    How to teach children twice as much.

    1. Teaching. I. Title.
LB1033.H32   372.1'102   73-11579
ISBN 0-87000-213-9

Contents

Preface

Every book should have a purpose. Mine is to tell an engaging tale which will, hopefully, alert the public to the machinations current in many American tax-supported school districts. Further, it is my desire to motivate some educators into trying a new and unique instructional technique which modifies pupil behavior so successfully that most students become responsible and self-reliant individuals.

My purpose is definitely not to hurt any person, but rather to improve the educational situation through improvement of its personnel and instructional techniques. Therefore, I have taken the liberty of changing names in the book whenever I felt that there was some possibility of injury.

I tried to stay as close to the facts as possible except where I portrayed my own conventional and Harrison System methods inside the classroom. Obviously I had to accelerate the time factor and perhaps overdramatize a few situations for the reader's enjoyment and to prevent boredom.

Allan E. Harrison

CHAPTER 1
The Morning
Conventional Teaching

A cold wave of fear passed down my spine despite the 90 degree temperature which is not unusual for September throughout the Southern California area. Not even a clear blue sky could raise my depression as I drove my old '54 Ford station wagon past the newly-plowed potato fields and toward the sixth grade classroom awaiting me at Sunnydale Elementary School.

Once again I nervously attempted to mentally tick off all the necessary items for a successful first day in the teaching profession. But, as in most moments of anguish and fear, my mind wouldn't function properly. I would have given anything at that moment to have returned to my old job as personnel specialist at the nearby Air Force base. However, such was not possible. My ties to the security of military service had been permanently severed in July and my future hitched to the uncertainty of teaching.

Just what caused me to make such a foolish decision escaped me at that time. Forgotten were the many miserable overtime hours, the stifled advancement opportunities, and even the initiative-killing Air Force regulations. Compared to the 35 ten and eleven-year old monsters I was about to face in the classroom, I felt that everything in the military had been a mere inconvenience. My imagination recently had many times pictured the poor helpless teacher, me, being driven from the classroom by a barrage of spitballs, unmanageable kids, angry parents and even the wrath of my principal.

To make matters worse, I had been unable to acquire, in the short three months available for summer school courses, any "how to teach" methods of instruction. Therefore, I was in the unenviable position of possessing knowledge without the foggiest idea of how to impart it to pupils. And to climax all, in the previous week I had listened to the usual new-teacher advice from every well-meaning veteran instructor who couldn't resist any opportunity to show off a bit of his classroom prowess. Several times I had been scared stiff as the helpful-teacher remarks went something like this: "Would you believe it? Only last year Mrs. Blank Blank was bitten twice, and the last time it was right on the breast by her kindergarten student." Great jumping jehosephat! I thought at the time. Where might the little devils get me?

Another motherly type of instructor kindly suggested that I immediately march any malcontent to the office by hanging on to the hair of his head. Another recommended a drawn circle on the blackboard into which the naughty pupil places his nose while standing on his tiptoes. But what probably frightened me the most were the dire warnings to avoid relying too much on the principal for discipline. "Handle it inside your classroom," everyone said.

I braked the station wagon to a stop in the school parking lot. Every step toward my classroom was dreadful with anticipation. Perhaps I could last a month and then surely the worst would be over. As I attempted to pull the classroom door open the kids swooped towards me. It seemed as if at least a hundred children were pushing while I was pulling. Actually, there were no more than fifteen or twenty. Finally I stopped pulling and the kids stopped pushing. I made a mental note to remember this strategy for later use.

"All right!" I yelled, above their chattering. "Line up and you can go inside one at a time." Surprisingly, they complied.

Hot dog! I thought. My first skirmish, and I had won. But my elation was short-lived. Once inside, I saw two boys trying to drag another from a choice desk seat at the back of the room. Classroom furniture was never designed for this and the desk upset with a loud bang. My first impulse was to rush over and knock some heads together, but I controlled myself with difficulty. What was it the books had said? A teacher must learn self-control before expecting it in others. But, as I was soon to discover, books were never written with my personality in mind. And after all, something had to be done right then. I asked myself: How would I handle this situation if it had occurred between my own three sons? The solution was immediately clear. The devil with books!

I rushed over and grabbed the two mischief-makers by the neck and hustled them out of the room. Once outside, I proceeded to give them a piece of my mind. But before I could do a good job, I heard further noises of disturbance coming from the classroom. I hurried inside. Instinctively, I knew the students were testing me. How I reacted now would determine my future success. Class discipline and control is the least taught but most sought subject in college. I had previously realized, as probably most new instructors have had to do in the past, that any expertise in classroom discipline would of necessity come from my experience in actual classroom combat. At least, this was always the evasive answer I received at college. Well the chance to learn was certainly and rapidly coming my way.

Inside the classroom, I understood the situation immediately. The chalkboard revealed the following derogatory statement: "JACKASS JOAN love DONKEY DAN." And evidently "Jackass Joan" was in hot pursuit of the male poet, up one aisle and down the other. Before I could reach them, the tall stringy blonde zeroed in and let fly with a large piece of chalk that bounced neatly off the head of her chubby quarry and then shattered against the wall.

I don't know what it was that stopped me as I started in pursuit. Probably the sudden realization that when the chips were down, and in the heat of excitement, I was acting no better than the kids I was supposed to change. Drawing again on my experience as a father, I tuned up my famous "bullhorn" voice and truly made the classroom windows rattle. "Stop your running, instantly! Freeze and don't move a muscle!"

The results frightened even me. All movement in the classroom came to a halt. Jaws hung open, and eyes widened. I quickly recovered my composure and made my voice as stern as possible.

"Out! Every one of you outside. If you are going to act like cattle, then you must rejoin the herd." I pointed toward the door for emphasis. "And don't come in again until the bell rings."

Surprisingly, they all left, meek as lambs. I felt a sigh of relief escape me after the last pupil had closed the door behind him. Here it was—reality staring me in the face. The experienced teachers had been right and the books wrong. All the old hands had warned, "Books won't help. Either you have the knack for classroom control or you don't. Those lacking it might just as well get out of teaching before they start, because successful discipline seldom arrives later." Without exception, the experienced instructor seemed to feel that failure breeds failure until all confidence is destroyed, at which time the teacher reverts to a mere information robot that doesn't care whether or not the pupil learns anything. He will blame his pupils, administrators and parents but never himself. I had already met a number of such robot instructors and felt a mixture of contempt and pity for them as they related class-room experiences. Contempt, in that they hadn't enough social con-science to retreat from teaching, and pity, in that such a move on their part was necessary for the children.

As I sat at my desk now, I mulled over the problem. Except for my God-given bullhorn voice, I might have become just such a teaching casualty. It didn't seem fair and it certainly wasn't logical. Many instructors possessed far more knowledge than the most successful disciplinarian, yet they were usually denied the pleasures and success expected in the profession. Perhaps there was a way to help these people. I felt that there would be a remedy which only experience and time would clarify. There just had to be!

The ringing of the school bell jarred me from my thoughts. The children filed into the room quietly and seated themselves with very little jockeying for favorite positions. Evidently the word had gone forth, as it has a strange way of doing among children everywhere. I watched their behavior with secret delight but my face wore the recommended opening day frown that is supposed to assure pupils that they are entering the Gates of Hell and that they must be on their best behavior while in the presence of the Devil. My fearsome countenance must have been effective for the silence remained even after the last child had been seated. Suddenly the realization hit me like a wet wash cloth. I was the teacher and these were my pupils. They had come to learn so it followed that I had to start teaching.

I groped among the materials on my desk for the lesson plan on which I had spent many painful hours the previous week. I just couldn't tear my eyes from the class. I felt that to do so might break the magic spell of tranquillity and plunge everything into chaos once more. Somehow, I forced my eyes to focus on the lesson plan. The pledge of allegiance and a song were scheduled first, followed by pupil introductions. It wasn't until the very end of the introductions that I began to really relax and enjoy myself. Then it was too late. My turn had arrived. I would *have* to begin teaching. Dear God, what should I do?

I found myself going through the motions mechanically. "Please take out your arithmetic book. Turn to page one. Who would like to do the first problem on the chalkboard? And the second? And the third?" I ran out of chalkboard space. I understood then why many teachers merely march methodically through the textbooks year after year. The line of least resistance is always easiest to take. I sat down at my desk to keep my knees from publicly entertaining the class. As I watched my pupils perform the required mathematical functions, my nerves relaxed enough to permit constructive thought. This doing by the students, rather than the teacher, seemed like a very productive approach to retentive learning, despite the possibility that it could be, and probably would be, considered a lazy teaching technique by many visiting principals. I decided that I would have to explore this possibility much further whenever my emotions allowed the luxury of innovative thinking within the classroom.

One thing had come as a surprise and yet shouldn't have. The children were as frightened as their teacher when it came time to perform before the whole class. In some way this fact seemed to soothe my own ragged emotions. It also gave rise to the realization that I needed more practice in classroom leadership. I was certain that with thought it could be accomplished. It took only a small amount of observation to discern how pitifully weak most pupils were in arithmetic basics. Some were counting on their fingers as they added. Others were adding columns of numbers instead of multiplying, and most students were completely bewildered at the mysteries of division. One little girl looked like she was about to cry until I quickly excused her. The tall stringy blonde called Joan, with the unerring chalk-throwing aim, declined to take her turn at the chalkboard.

Finally, I could stand it no longer and gave them all a timed speed test in each of the basics. My shock at the results was profound. How could textbook authorities expect children to do any mathematics with as little basic skill as my class demonstrated? Surely, as a novice instructor, I had not been handed the mentally retarded in this school.

I desperately tried to inject some enthusiasm into some drill practices, without success. Secretly, I sympathized with my pupils' obvious agony. Drill was a bitter medicine almost impossible to sugar-coat. It was little wonder that previous teachers of this class had given up from frustration and weariness. Nevertheless, the seriousness of this teaching failure demanded persistence and further investigation. If I were ever to become successful as a teacher of arithmetic, the motivation problem in basics had to be solved.

"All right. Put your math away," I said, finally, unable to keep the frustration from my voice. "Let's try some English. Perhaps you're better in this area. Turn to page six in your textbook."

Surprisingly, the pupils tried to accomplish something. Just why they should try, or even want to try, seemed a mystery to me. But I realized that usually the top 20 or 30 percent of a class was eager to display the academic prowess it possessed despite the pain and embarrassment it caused to most of the others. At least that was the way it was when I went to school many years earlier. So what drove all of the rest? Fear of me, perhaps? It seemed logical, since pleasure was obviously missing from their expressions. What an unhealthy situation, I thought.

I paused in my inspection efforts, as I walked around the room looking over my pupils' shoulders. The cute little blonde girl to whom I spoke would probably fall into the category of teacher's pet in most classrooms—anxious to please and definitely a good student. She answered my question with enthusiasm. "Oh yes! I like grammar a real lot."

I winced inwardly and picked up her paper to examine the errors I knew were there. I wasn't surprised. Lack of basic knowledge seemed universal. If such a deficiency existed in one of my best pupils, who liked grammar, what talent must reside in the rest of the class?

I spoke loud enough for all to hear. "Close your books and take out a clean sheet of paper. I want you to write the eight parts of speech and describe what each does."

Blank stares came from all parts of the room. A few pupils went through the motions of compliance. An example was evidently in order. The only thing that I could bring to mind, at the moment, was the definition for a noun, which I promptly gave. Fortunately, this appeared to be sufficient. The class looked busy again. I hurried to my desk and sat down, weak from the fearsome realization that my own training in grammar was rudimentary. Therefore, was it fair or reasonable to expect more of my pupils? Where had my own instructors failed? Or had they? Didn't the real secret of correct grammar lie in its habitual use? But, how could anyone acquire such a desirable habit? These questions shouted for an answer but none came. Somewhere in the realm of my past or future experience lay the answer. But of one thing I was certain: it would need to come soon or my teaching days were over. My nerves were never built for this kind of frustration.

As the pupils began to put their completed work on my desk, I gave an assignment in the reading textbook—a state reader furnished to all California school districts. I studied the youthful faces around the room as they silently labored with the words. Lip readers were abundant. Some pupils seemed to read efficiently and effortlessly, as their eyes darted from words to words. Whether or not there was any retention was another thing. Some were what I later came to call "pick 'n pokers." It was all I could do to refrain from physically curtailing such infantile and ineffective finger pointing. Didn't they realize how much their finger slowed them down? I glanced at my list of pupil names. "John Smith! Would you please begin reading orally at the top of page 21?"

John pushed himself to his feet and began. It was apparent that he had been taught with the look-and-say method. Whenever he came to an unfamiliar word, John would patiently wait for me to pronounce it.

I urged him to attempt some on his own but with little success. Finally, I asked Mary Brown to continue. There was a shocked and pained silence for almost thirty seconds.

"Mary Brown! Please stand up and read." I said with firmness.

A small girl in the back of the room arose slowly. Even from where I sat I could see the tears starting to form. Hurriedly I tried to rectify the error. "You may sit down, Mary. Perhaps you can read later, when you see that there is no reason to be afraid."

"She ain't afraid! It's just that she's like me and can't read," piped up our classroom poet whose head still carried a small visible lump from the previously thrown chalk.

I sighed disgustedly as most of the class laughed. I had heard that every classroom contained at least one clown. Evidently mine was no exception. I let the remark pass without comment rather than expose little Mary Brown to further embarrassment. However I felt the necessity of discovering how many more literary cripples the room contained.

"Please put up your hand if you feel that you are a poor reader," I said.

To my surprise, over half of the class had hands in the air. There must be some mistake, I thought. Either my predecessors had been very derelict or else my pupils were hoping to be excused from any further oral reading by such chicanery. By randomly calling upon pupils to read, I soon discovered that my worst fears were well founded. About half of my students could be classified as poor readers. Then again, maybe my own standards were too high. I would remember to ask some of my colleagues about this at recess.

Smoke in the teachers' lounge was thicker than a garage fire to which I had been summoned as a fireman in my younger days. I sat down beside a nicotine puffer and unhappily resigned myself to the inhalation of the foul vapor in the interest of instructional progress. "Mrs. Jones, does your sixth grade class contain as many poor readers as mine? I was wondering if my own standards were just too high."

Mrs. Jones smiled before gulping her coffee in such a way that her inhaled cigarette smoke was never expelled. Her lungs must be as black as the La Brea Tar Pits, I thought. "About a third to a half of the average sixth grade class in California has reading difficulties," she said. "I have over half my sixth grade in third through fifth readers and I would go even lower than this except for the time it takes to work with such a large grade spread."

We continued talking for another fifteen minutes but for the life of me I couldn't remember what was said. The initial shock of her first statement left me dazed. The bell rang and I headed for my classroom convinced of two things. California schoolchildren were not being taught to read and too many elementary teachers were nicotine addicts. Perhaps one was the cause of the other, but which was the cause would be hard to say.

I was greeted at the schoolroom door with new confrontations generated by the freeplay allowed at recess time. Our classroom's tall and thin chalk-thrower was sobbing in her hands while most of the gathered crowd tried to explain what had happened. But the cacophonous sound made intelligent understanding impossible. I managed to get the door open and motioned my pupils inside. It took several minutes to calm the class. Meanwhile, I refused to hear any complaints or explanations until silence reigned—this was a textbook technique. After glancing at my class roster, I said, "Joan, would you please tell me what happened?"

A half dozen voices began answering instead.

I stood up and silenced them with a wave of my hand. "Are all of you called Joan? Please let Joan explain." Joan uncovered her tear-filled eyes, revealing a fat lump on one eyebrow. "Henry socked me in the eye!" she sobbed.

Henry's reply from the other side of the room was loud, angry, and instantaneous. "She called me a nigger!"

The room turned to an icy silence. Only the deep breathing of the few asthmatic pupils could be heard. Oh dear, I thought fearfully, here it was on my first day. Why couldn't the racial issue have waited until I had acquired a little more experience in handling such delicate matters? Well it hadn't, so I would have to blunder through.

"You shouldn't have called Henry a 'nigger.' People of his race wish to be addressed as Negro or black."

I had intended to continue but Danny, our classroom clown and poet, cut me off. "Why is that, Mr. Harrison? Anybody can see that Henry ain't black. In fact he ain't even brown. He's more like a grey. And I even knew one 'nigger' down South that was red, at least his hair was."

This brought immediate laughter from the class and Henry to his feet. "You want a fat lump too, Danny darling?" Henry's brown eyes shot fire. I stood up immediately and motioned Henry back into his seat. "Sit down Henry! And Danny, your comments were not asked. So please don't speak out again unless I call on you."

"That's the trouble," Danny retorted. "Nobody ever calls on me, unless it's to read or do some other stupid thing where I look like a jackass."

Again the class laughed. This time I speared Danny with wintery eyes. "That's enough, or I'll have to send you from the room." Much to my shame, I felt an urge to hurt. "Just remember, Danny, there is an old saying that goes like this: It is better to keep mouth closed and be thought a fool than to open it and confirm the fact."

"That's me all right—an open-mouth fool." The clown in him couldn't resist despite the risk. Recognizing this, I ignored the classroom smiles and continued. "Now Joan, will you please tell us why you called Henry a name you knew he wouldn't like?"

"He wouldn't give up his seat in the swing when his time was up." The rest of the class backed her statement with a chorus of similar assertions.

I felt trapped. How could I render a clear-cut decision when both were at fault. Yet the problem demanded a solution, at once. I quickly, but fruitlessly, searched my conscience for a satisfactory answer. Being human, I decided that the best course was to sweep the dilemma under the rug if possible. No solution was better than a wrong or unjust one, I rationalized.

"Since you were both in the wrong, my hands are tied. Therefore, I want you both to apologize to each other and the issue will be dropped immediately." I cringed inwardly. What a cowardly and unsatisfactory way to settle anything! Neither damaged party had received any real satisfaction. This undesirable situation had to be put high on my list of things demanding a remedy. And on top of everything else, even that paragon of virtue, their classroom teacher, had not come through this encounter with clean hands. How could I expect to instruct young minds in proper behavior when I could not control my own emotions? My inexcusable anger at Danny was still shamefully clear. Yes, a solution to these classroom problems of emotional control and maturity would carry a high priority for the future. Fortunately for all concerned, both Henry and Joan apologized as asked. I shuddered to think of what I might have done if they had refused.

The subject of spelling was introduced next. And again, the lack of basic phonics was painfully clear. Most of my pupils seemed incapable of sounding out words and what was worse, few could be induced to try.

Just before lunch another typical classroom problem arose. Little Gladys Horner couldn't find her pencil and complained to me. This was more serious than it sounds. I had been previously informed that teachers are constantly plagued with missing educational tools—lost, stolen, misplaced pencils, books, etc. This, I knew, would stop any class cold, as it had now stopped mine.

"Has anyone seen Gladys' pencil?" I asked, and received no reply. "Well, who has one that she may borrow?" The silence was deafening. Finally, dear Danny could restrain himself no longer. "Nobody's going to lend her one. We never get it back. She must take 'em home and sell 'em."

"Now that wasn't nice, Danny," I admonished. "Please apologize to Gladys."

"Aw, all right. I'm sorry that you're the way you are, Gladys." He grinned as the rest of the class laughed.

"I'll have no more of your facetiousness or you're going straight to the principal!" I bellowed. Then I could have bitten my tongue, I was that sorry. I knew, as most new teachers do, that much of the novice instructor's classroom effectiveness is gauged by the disciplinary control he enjoys. Knowing Danny's nature, I had just handed my principal his first weapon for my dismissal. The boy's natural proclivity for trouble would require frequent referrals. I gave little Gladys Horner my own pencil and wearily sat down to worry about the undesirable situation into which I had inadvertently placed myself.

The lunch bell jarred me from horrible speculations. I waved the kids outside and continued with my gloomy reflections. But suddenly I became aware of Danny still seated at his desk. He raised his hand while his round fat face carried a smile. "Mr. Harrison, what's facelessness mean?"

My jaw dropped open, revealing my perplexity. "Gosh, Danny, I don't know. Where did you hear that?"

"From you," he said, still trying to smile, but not knowing whether he should or not. "Heck, Mr. Harrison, I try to show my emotions on my face as much as I can."

Suddenly the light dawned and I laughed. "No, no, Danny! Facetiousness means that you are trying to be funny or amusing."

"Oh!" Danny exclaimed as he headed for the door, plainly happy once again. "That's all right then. That dumb 'Pinhead,' who sits next to me, said he would bet that it was some kind of high-powered and polite cussword. But if it just means funny there's no sense in my trying to remember it, since I'm just naturally that."

As the door swung shut I laughed out loud. How could teachers hate even the unruly kids?

CHAPTER 2
The Afternoon
Conventional Teaching

I gobbled my lunch right along with my children. A half hour to eat didn't seem long enough to me. But it appeared more than sufficient for the playground-bound kids and my dying-for-a-smoke colleagues. I noticed that a few teachers had developed the ability to unwind and relax at that time. Perhaps I could emulate their technique.

"Let's go, Al! It's almost 12:30. Mr. Turner is pretty much of a stickler on punctuality." This statement jarred me from my speculations. Joe Coble, a fifth grade instructor, was offering a kindly reminder that we had a fifteen-minute tour of playground duty together. The fierce summer heat hit me in the face as we walked to a shady area behind the buildings where we could observe most of the playground. The two female teachers we relieved thanked us and left.

What a waste of human energy, I thought, as I trudged back to my classroom. The slight breeze blowing on the back of my damp shirt soothed my hot exasperation. It seemed foolish, to say the least, to require baby sitting service from highly educated instructors when many parents would enjoy such a position if they were employed at a small salary.

Well, I wondered as I approached my own classroom, what would be my fortune for the afternoon session? Could I last out the day before disaster struck? As I came closer, I certainly had my doubts. A group of ten or fifteen children stood observantly in front of my door, watching a heated argument between Danny and Henry. Before I could get there, Henry grabbed Danny by the front of his shirt. Danny's pudgy face had turned chalky and Henry's was twisted in a snarl, his brown eyes flashing pits of fire as he spat out his ultimatum. "If you ever call me that again, I'll beat you to a bloody pulp!"

I tore Henry's hand loose and stepped between them. "All right! That's enough of that! Both of you go into the classroom and cool off."

Since Danny appeared more than pleased to obey and Henry acted just the opposite, I turned my attention to him. All of my 180 pounds stood between Henry and the object of his anger, but this seemed of no consequence as he advanced. I clamped my work-hardened hands onto Henry's upper arms. I felt Henry's muscles strain and tense under my strong grip, as he struggled to release himself. But despite his considerable strength he was no match for mine, which had recently been developed through the strenuous exercise involved in building my own house.

"Let me go! Take your hands off me!" Henry raged. "My Dad'll fix you good."

I saw red, instantly. I lifted Henry clear off the ground and shook him until his head flopped from side to side and his eyes opened wide with fear. The whites contrasted sharply with the grey of his face as I lowered him to his feet once more.

"Now go into the classroom," I bellowed, "And I don't want to hear a peep out of you or anyone else until I ask for it."

If the building had been on fire I am certain that every one of my pupils would not have moved faster, including Henry. Even the children from other classes scurried toward their rooms when I turned my attention toward them. My own classroom had tomb-like qualities as I hurried inside and sat down at my desk. To hide the nervous reaction I felt approaching, I fussed with the material in one of the bottom drawers. Over the quietness of the room, I again heard the breathing of my asthmatic students. I was also aware of the many sweaty bodies crammed into our twenty by thirty-foot room. If this was teaching, I wanted no more. Anyway, after Mr. Turner, my principal, received the details of my recent adventure, there would be little need to worry about whether or not I wanted to teach. I wondered, what kind of employment opportunities existed for fired instructors? Were they like old elephants who wandered off to die in obscurity?

The subject of dying activated a thought on living. There remained the rest of the day through which I had to manage to live before my carcass could be buried. I lifted my eyes up from the desk drawer and looked around the classroom. All the pupils had been watching, but now each was anxious to pretend that he or she hadn't.

"Take out your social studies textbook and turn to page seven."
I hoped my inner turmoil wasn't too obvious.

Most pupils hurried to comply and had little time for observation of me. Evidently one demonstration of my displeasure was enough for one day. What an awful way to run a classroom, I thought. Fear as a motivator is the worst of educational tools. Yet it seemed, at the time, to be the only effective one available to elementary school teachers. Something had to be done and soon, I thought, or our nation would pay a terrible price. Wouldn't it be wonderful if children liked classes so much that they refused to go out to play? Just think of the problems this would solve.

Only then did I recall where I was and become aware of the social studies textbook open before me. I had to hold my mind in check and tend to the business at hand.

"John! Would you please read the first three paragraphs on page seven?"

John complied, and was followed by a ten minute classroom discussion of the material. Sally Butler read next, and again I attempted to involve pupils in an imaginary visit to the outside world. Wouldn't it be great if, instead, the teacher could grab life itself and drag a slice into the classroom for the kids to actually enjoy?

Read and discuss. Read and discuss. This is the way it went for the next half hour. Some "how to teach" textbooks I had read recommended this as one proper procedure, but the boredom of the process wasn't mentioned.

(Another textbook technique was to induce students to make imaginary excursions into the outside world. Reports were written. In my classroom, it seemed to fail miserably. Perhaps I was at fault, especially in my present mood, but I couldn't believe the reason resided solely there. Finally, in desperation, I consigned the whole class to previously devised study groups, another recommended technique, which seemed, at first, to hold their interest. Slowly their curiosity waned as the newness wore off. Minor discipline problems reared their ugly heads.)

As I watched, the class pretended to be busy. My mind roamed the social studies field for other possible solutions. The subject of social studies is vast, perhaps too vast, and the fault could lie there. How could anyone expect a child to experience much in all of its many divisions, let alone retain it?

Promptly the idea was there, teasing me. Experience! Wasn't experience the best of all teachers? Why not use experience? But how? Could this be accomplished in a way that would be meaningful and motivational to children? Certainly, most people would agree that the painful mistakes suffered as an adult belonged in the classroom where they could be dissected and studied for future remedial action. But again, how could this be achieved on a child's level?

I had been so engrossed in my idea, that I had failed to notice the laughter until it became excessively loud. Harry Haddock had June Snively's shoe off and was tickling her foot.

"Stop that, Harry!" I yelled.

All movement in the room ceased immediately. Breaths were held in anticipation of the forthcoming cyclonic explosion.

"Everybody move back to your own seat and put your textbook away," I said just as calmly as I could. "I am going to give you all a quiz on the material we have covered. Those pupils who fail to achieve an acceptable score will take their paper home and have it signed by a parent to indicate that they have seen it. Further, these students will also do homework in the subject tonight."

A groan escaped the class, but they went about the business of complying. Sheets of lined paper appeared, and also pencils, without any request from me. I felt dirty inside. Once again, fear had to be used. And I even had to exploit parental authority to get the job done. If I still had a teaching position tomorrow, this situation called for an immediate remedy. Just what, escaped me at the time.

I gave the quiz in an autocratic style and manner which most instructors would brand as acceptable. Next, I collected all examinations and *began* a hurried correction, while the class was ordered to read silently the first chapter in their science textbook. *Began* was the proper word, for the task was almost beyond human accomplishment. First one child and then another was at my desk seeking reading assistance. Finally the line grew to six or seven. In desperation, I warned them all to stay away until I finished correcting their test papers or I would eat them alive.

This was the worst of teaching practices and I knew it. How could pupils learn without the necessary help? But I felt trapped by my previous ultimatum on homework and took the line of least resistance. Why in the world couldn't students ever exercise just a little bit of self-reliance and help one another? Instantly, the thought fell on me like a bear at a bee hive. That was it! One reason for many classroom difficulties was *lack of self-reliance!* I almost choked with excitement as I said the phrase to myself once more. Why had I been so stupid? I should have seen the reason for this right away.

Almost without exception, elementary school classrooms, within my experience, operated as benevolent dictatorships in which the instructors ran everything. In fact, if teachers did not do just that, the accusation was usually made that they had no control of their kids, and I knew that few teachers care for that label. Most instructors act with the absolute authority that brings forth such praise as: "She has no discipline problems," or "See how quiet her room is; the kids learn a lot in there."

But how was it possible for much self-reliance to grow in such an atmosphere? From past bitter memories, I recalled the consequences of being different from the herd. What chance did any budding Edison or Winston Churchill have in today's elementary school where teachers were so busy making everyone equal?

Today's elementary school? Was the classroom really much different in the past? Didn't Abraham Lincoln face the same bleak repression of the self-reliance he could exercise? Yes, he did, I imagined, but probably only *inside* the classroom. In Lincoln's day, all pupils graduated into some semblance of a free enterprise society where self-reliance was prized and necessary for survival. This effectively erased the classroom-instilled concept of "all for the state" (meaning the teacher), "and the state for all."

This would also explain our nation's gradual drift toward more and more governmental control. Students, conditioned for twelve to sixteen years in a classroom atmosphere of directed activity, would be likely to expect and even demand the same regulation from their government in times of difficulty. The picture was crystal clear, and it frightened me. Our schools unwittingly had become tools for enslavement. The forces of dictatorship, and communism, need do nothing in this country to succeed. It was insidiously being accomplished within the classroom.

Facts, as they exist today, then fell into an intelligible whole. Welfare as a way of life. A rising crime rate. Increased use of drugs. Devil cults and riots. When people were robbed of self-reliance training, they could be as easily led by forces of evil as they could by good. Children who had little opportunity to think for themselves in the classroom shouldn't be expected to do so as an adult. With such an educational product as this coming from our schools, it would be easy for any influential person to gather them into a mob. These nonthinkers would probably foolishly demand to be controlled in the interest of the security and dependence they enjoyed previously as students. Only after the deed was done would they realize their mistake.

"Mr. Harrison! Mr. Harrison!" No one but Danny would have had the audacity to disturb me after my previous warning.

Danny stood beside my desk and tugged at my shirt sleeve for attention. "Mr. Harrison! I can't read this science junk unless you help me. Couldn't John pronounce the word for me whenever I get stuck?"

Excellent idea, I thought. This would provide enough necessary assistance to let me finish my corrections.

"Sure, Danny," I smiled. I stood up and announced that the better pupils could help the slower students whenever necessary. The news was well received and helped to relax the strain and tension I had previously created. As pupil helped pupil, an equal opportunity existed that was missing before. Pleased with the apparent results, I returned to my reflections and corrections.

This classroom procedure of "each one teach one" worked very successfully in the one-room schoolhouse. Why not apply its principles to modern education? The opportunity to teach leadership qualities in the classroom rather than just on the ball diamond was an exciting thought indeed. And just imagine the academic progress that would be possible if instant help were available to every student in all subjects. Visions of three years' academic achievement for my pupils in just months swam before my eyes. But suddenly the vision was shattered by shouts from the back of the room.

"I'm going to tell Mr. Harrison that you won't help me!" Danny exclaimed to John, who sat across from him.

"Aw, you want help all the time," John replied loudly, probably as much for my benefit as Danny's. "I can't get my own work done for helping you."

"All right, boys. That'll be enough." I turned to look at Susie who sat on the other side of Danny. "Susie! Would you please help Danny whenever he needs assistance?"

Upon receiving Susie's nod of acquiescence, I returned to my corrections and speculations. That little episode demonstrated quite clearly why the technique of student assistance was not more widely employed. The reason for John's refusal to help could be assigned to a lack of motivation. He could see little personal reward coming to him, either in the aesthetic joy of doing the act, or in compensation that could be spent later. His situation, I realized, was unique to say the least. As an adult teacher, I helped pupils in my classroom for two reasons. I was paid to do so and I enjoyed it. However, I had to be honest and admit that if there had been no pay in the beginning I never could have been induced to teach for the joy of it alone. Yet, isn't this exactly what I had expected from John? Now that I mulled it over in my mind, it seemed pure nonsense. How could pupils too young even to understand the basic drives of nature be expected to value an education?

Suddenly, the test paper I was checking jerked me back into the world of reality. Even the automatic checking procedure I had adopted to finish the task in time wouldn't permit this to pass. It was obvious even to my inexperienced eye that Henry had flagrantly cheated. Oh dear! I thought. Not another conflagration like the last one. My nerves wouldn't stand it even if Henry's muscular body could. Cheating, in my mind, was another disorder that seemed to fall at the doorstep of autocratic teaching methods. I have always felt that cheating is a device of the weak to reduce competition. Since each pupil competes constantly for the limited attention of the benevolent dictator it follows that cheating, in the child's mind, is the fastest route to a place in the sun.

Healthy competition, I felt, never hurt anyone. However, it must be available on a voluntary basis where there is equal opportunity for all. I knew of no conventional classroom where this existed, including my own. So the problem became knottier. What could and should be done with Henry? This problem required far more thought and time than I could give it then. So once again, I was very human and took the line of least resistance. I set Henry's paper to one side and finished correcting the few I had left.

I stood up and announced, "Everyone turn his science textbook to page thirteen. Please notice the experiment there. I will now attempt to perform this in front of the class."

I went through the proper procedures and received the correct results along with the oh's and ah's of my youthful observers. How much more effective it would have been, I surmised, if a pupil had performed it instead of me. But at the time this seemed unlikely. I had been forewarned by a number of my older and wiser colleagues not to allow such a thing to happen. "They'll pour the plaster of Paris down the sink," some said.

So for the present I did the experiment myself. However, I was determined that if there were more, I would find a way to involve my students. Real retention, I knew, went with trying to teach something to others. Upon completing the demonstration, I returned to my desk and picked up the pile of social studies examination papers. "Susie, as a reward for helping Danny, you may pass these papers back to the class." Susie beamed her delight as she performed the task.

And then it started. First one pupil and then another complained about the grade I had given. Wasn't this correct? Or what about that answer in the book: it meant the same thing as he or she had on the paper, didn't it? And how about Larry's paper? You didn't mark his wrong like you did mine. Also, you gave Ray a B-minus and I got the same number right and only received a C-plus.

My nerves cried out for relief. I wanted to tell them all to shut up and sit down. After all, who had a better right? Wasn't I the dictator in my own room, and if I wanted to fail them all, who was there to say that I couldn't? Only my own sense of justice, I decided. Therefore, I tried hard to explain and rationalize. Finally in desperation I gave up.

"All right! Shut up and sit down!" I yelled, pointing toward their seats. "Give me just a minute to think about what I'm going to do."

I sat down at my desk and cradled my chin in my hands and stared blankly at the class while the class stared back. The room was incredibly quiet. Even my asthmatic pupils seemed to be holding their breath. At last the ridiculousness of the situation swept over all of us at about the same time. A few of the more bold students grinned at me and I found myself grinning back. Finally I laughed, and that broke the ice. My pupils laughed with me.

After a few moments I held out my hands, palm downward, and waved them up and down. This brought the room back to some semblance of order. Still grinning, I said, "I guess the first day of school is pretty much of a nervous strain on everybody and it takes a good laugh to clear the air." I became more serious now, but I still couldn't keep just a little smile from the corners of my mouth. "Perhaps I have acted too much like a tyrant today, but I'm sure you will agree there were times when you needed it. However, by way of making amends, I'll abrogate the social studies homework requirement."

To my surprise, nobody seemed pleased. Instead, most of the class looked slightly shocked. In the end, it took Danny's boldness to set the situation straight. "What's that mean? Are you going to give us some more?"

I couldn't keep back the smile. I had momentarily forgotten that these were sixth graders. "No, Danny. It means that I'm going to do away with it entirely."

That brought the house down. Claps, whistles, and yells of approval echoed off the walls. I quickly motioned them back to order for fear of a visit from the principal. As I did so, I silently recognized myself for what I was, a pedagogical coward who again had taken the easy way out of a difficult classroom situation.

I knew that homework is the nightmare of most classrooms, and that grades are devilishly hard to handle properly. Many instructors had secretly confessed to me that homework and grades are far more trouble than they are ever worth. For instance: pupils fail to accomplish the evening assignment because of the inability of parents to help, which brings the teacher criticism; the teacher must spend many home hours correcting completed work; and the nervous strain and tension at report card time is terrible. But many instructors and pupils endure worse experiences daily with grades which exist as the sole reward or punishment in some classrooms.

And to think that here, at one masterful stroke, I had escaped from the pit I had dug with the social studies examination. I should have been elated but instead I felt that I had cheated my students. Someday, if I stayed in the teaching profession, I wanted to do something about homework and grades. I felt certain that many people would be pleased.

The dismissal bell was a welcome sound to everyone. The children put away their educational materials and I waved an arm at the door signifying that they could leave. My students weren't the type that needed the second invitation. A mass of bodies flowed toward the door and outside. I could hear them whooping and hollering as they raced down the sidewalk. I winced inwardly at the mistake I had made. Just one more example of the missing self-reliance, I thought.

I slumped exhausted into my chair. Then, as soon as I touched the seat, I remembered. My time of doom had arrived! I had to rouse myself and report the day's adventures to my principal, Mr. Turner, before Henry's parents could. Each step toward the office gave me less and less courage. Perhaps I should wait until tomorrow. Maybe Henry's parents would never call. If I waited, at least I could look forward to one more day of teaching. One more day of teaching? Was I crazy? The memories of the last six hours flooded over me. I had to be out of my head even to think of asking for any more. No, there were too many things that I had to get straight to permit any procrastination. It was now or never.

Mr. Turner was about my height, weight and age—five feet nine, one hundred and seventy pounds, and pushing thirty-three. This assured me that he wouldn't get violent. He sat at his big mahogany desk and listened intently as I related the various events of the day. His friendly blue eyes twinkled merrily with understanding, and he occasionally smoothed his thinning light brown hair whenever I revealed some portion of the story that made me look particularly bad. Once he even smiled as he leaned back in his swivel chair. Other teachers had warned me that I was due for a shock whenever this happened. Mr. T's smile changed him into an entirely different person, they had said. He seemed so warm and friendly while it lasted that he could have dismissed me on the spot and I would have probably shook his hand. Finally I finished with my sad tale and I was rewarded with his thousand dollar smile. "Well," he said. "If that's the only trouble you've had on your first day, I'll say that you're going to make a fine instructor."

I wanted to reach over and hug him but contented myself with shaking his hand. "Thank you very much, Mr. T." My mile wide grin disappeared instantly with the slip of my tongue. My frustration was acute. "I'm sorry, Mr. Turner, I shouldn't have called you 'Mr. T.' "

His high-priced smile was there. "That's all right. Just call me Roy, except in front of the children."

I left his office with a warm glow. If all teachers had a boss like that, I couldn't imagine why they would ever want to quit. Now I could go home and put the old brain to work on some of the teaching ideas which had been buzzing around in my head. I began to whistle as I walked toward my car and paid no attention at all to the 105 degree afternoon heat.

CHAPTER 3
Philosophies
Dreams for the System

I arrived at my classroom two hours before the morning bell was scheduled to ring. This surely would provide sufficient thinking time with no student interruptions. To assure myself of this, I locked the door immediately after entering. I sat down in my chair, tilted it back, locked my hands behind my head, and then put one foot after the other upon my desk. It was a comfortable position for me, and was conducive to deep thought. I had to bring together the many ideas that had been chasing around in my mind.

Since most conventional methods of teaching were forms of benevolent dictatorships, it was reasonable to assume that nothing less than the opposite techniques would erase the harmful effects. But I also realized that unlimited freedom was not the answer. Anarchy seldom solved anything. Something in between, which leaned heavily upon democratic and free enterprise principles, would be ideal. But whatever I used, it had to contain the *opportunity* for every student to exercise self-reliance in a reward and punishment atmosphere. In other words, the system had to allow each pupil to experience life on a miniature scale in such a way that it would be meaningful and encourage him to learn more.

That was it! The realization struck me so hard that I almost fell off the chair. Why not use our own capitalistic nation as a guide? Was there ever a country more successful in history? Economically, we had the highest standard of living in the world. It seemed an ideal pattern to copy inside the classroom. To be certain that I was right, I began a systematic analysis of my idea.

Some form of monetary reward had to be used which would be

meaningful and motivational. The plan had to teach values that children could and should use. Also the system had to occasionally include the concept of duty without reward. And above all, it would need to emphasize the evil of the love of money. All this seemed, at the moment, to be a very tall order.

First, to accomplish such goals, instruction in desirable social values would be included. All of society would be upgraded by the program. The new system of teaching would permit children to make mistakes and then offer the opportunity to rectify them. With a new method, pupils could learn to become responsible for their actions and pay the penalty for errors. This seemed to me a vital ingredient missing in the conventional classroom. As a conventional teacher, I was constantly trying to keep my pupils from making mistakes. Yet blunders are remembered by students equally as long as successes. Why cheat children of an essential part of their education?

Second, the new system would require that desirable economic values be taught. Most adults not in business have almost no concept of practical finance. This, I felt, came from a lack of instruction when it could have been the most easily accomplished—inside the classroom. How many people, I thought, understand the desirability of thrift or circumspect purchasing, let alone any methods for saving or buying? Not many, I was sure, if marriage counselors could be believed. About half the divorces today are caused by mismanaged finances.

In my fantasy classroom, children would be able to experience life in economic areas at their level of understanding. This would allow them to cope effectively with similar situations as adults. And after all, isn't this what the education of the young is all about?

Third, my innovative techniques would have personal values automatically built into them. Attitudes, desires, philosophies and characters would be shaped through experience and, I hoped, retained forever. As students worked closely with each other, respect for strengths and weaknesses would come. This could be induced by giving each child a vested interest in the success of others.

Probably the most important concept that would be in my proposal was the one that triggered it in the first place—self-reliance. The idea of something for nothing would be completely erased and children would be taught to think for themselves. Mistakes would be costly in some way besides the motherly cluckings of the benevolent teacher.

Pupils would be forced to undergo instructional experiences in race relationships, government, and business that would fill voids now existing in conventional classrooms. Other neglected instruction would also be offered, such as: training in the best way to handle competition; opportunities to enjoy pleasures and hobbies that would combat the growing trend toward the pseudo-pleasures of drugs, crime, sex, etc.; and finally, children would experience relationships with each other that would encourage leadership within the classroom rather than just at the ball diamond.

The further I pondered the educational needs of my pupils the more vast the task seemed. However, one fact was glaringly apparent: present teaching methods were woefully inadequate. From the standpoint of the instructor, my new system would need to lessen the tension and nervous strain. I had heard that many of my colleagues go home at night to tranquillizers and strong drink. The innovative methods had also to reduce the petty details required of the instructor.

I knew it wouldn't take much to demonstrate the success of my project. The achievement from most classrooms was so little that the janitor probably could accomplish as much. On second thought, using the janitor might not be such a bad idea! Many of today's teachers have become so indoctrinated with the love of learning that their students receive too much and turn off. A noninstructor, entering such a classroom, might spot the problem at once. For instance, the janitor would probably realize that learning is work, and that children can only absorb so much. Homework, after a hard day in the classroom, often has the reverse effect from that desired. Sometimes little learning takes place at home and then the youngsters are too tired the next day to learn much. Therefore, if possible, homework should be eliminated in my new system. With daytime motivation at its peak, homework seemed unnecessary.

Academic improvements for pupils would come only if certain techniques could be developed. As an example, instant aid for the slow would have to be available; all day learning would have to take place for proper retention; cheating would be reduced; and the pressure on pupils would be eliminated through self-motivation and self-discipline.

The program I had in mind would be, in fact had to be, implemented piecemeal. I realized that any other course would swamp the teacher. The vastness of what I was proposing sent my head into a whirl. But I also knew that it was necessary, for education has too long resorted to instructional bandaids which actually accomplish little. Perhaps my proposal, even then, wasn't large enough.

Every day overworked teachers were being driven from the schoolhouse with petty classroom details that might better be performed by their pupils who could profit from the experience. Parents were asked to teach their children at home when knowledgeable help was available from eager pupils who lived nearby. Society was seeing less and less creativity coming from the classroom. These defects, and many more, cried out for remedies. My new system had to solve them to be called successful. But I was also acutely aware of the vast difference between discovering problems and finding their solutions.

My head ached from all this heavy thinking. Gradually I became aware of the playground noise outside, but it wasn't until the bell began clanging above my head that I roused myself and opened the door. I felt that my two-hour analysis had been time well spent. Capitalism in the classroom would be an excellent tool to accomplish most of the objectives I had in mind.

CHAPTER 4

The Second Day

Basics for Starting the System

As my pupils straggled in from the playground and gradually settled in their seats, I thumbed nervously through the dittoed stack of papers on my desk with the hope that I had a sufficient supply. I had run off over a hundred last evening. These were class roster sheets with small squares beside each name for grade score entries. If my plans were correct, these rosters would become a major tool in my newly designed system.

It was seven minutes before most students settled down and eight minutes before I could talk to my class in a conversational manner. Alterations were in order, I thought to myself. This amount of time lost each recess was unthinkable.

"Good morning, students!" I said calmly, hoping that my inner agitation was not too apparent. "We are going to embark upon a brand new system today. To some of you it may seem like a game of 'Monopoly.' From now on you will enjoy school."

This brought forth audible reactions of disbelief and derision. I waited patiently for the noise to subside before continuing. "The first thing we will do is eliminate grades, except at report card time."

Again the students spontaneously reacted, but this time affirmatively and louder than before. My irritation grew with the volume. I decided that maybe the only thing the students of today understood *was* either force or fear, and I detested both. I have always felt that teachers should use such weapons only in an emergency. Well, as far as I was concerned, the emergency was here and now.

"All right! That's enough!" I bellowed loud enough to raise Danny and about half the class six inches off their seat. "The next one I hear flapping his fat rubber lip will spend the morning recess writing."

Pins could have been dropped and would have sounded like the plucking of a harp string.

"That's better!" I said, relaxing my features just a little. "Now, as I was saying before, grades will be given only at report card time." I speared Danny with a wintery eye to prevent his asking the question I could see forming inside his restless soul. Surprisingly, it worked, and Danny swallowed hard to keep from speaking. I continued, "Instead of academic grades, you will earn points or rather make-believe 'classroom dollars' for all academic work. These classroom dollars can be accumulated and deposited in the schoolroom bank where each pupil will have his or her own bank account."

Danny could restrain himself no longer. "Can I use these classroom dollars to pay my old man so he won't swat my fanny at report card time?"

Naturally, this put the class into hysterics.

I waved the room into some approximation of order before spearing Danny with a fiery eye. "Danny, this system is going to be designed for clowns just like you. Every classroom has one and I am quite certain that I would have died from shame if mine had been an exception. The rascals of every class manage to drive the instructor to do either of two things: The teacher becomes a tyrant and snatches pupils bald-headed for the slightest infraction, or the instructor retreats inside a shell and trains himself to ignore almost everything outside of it. By using the system, neither of these things need happen, and certainly won't to me. We will cry together when you force me to take your money for infractions of the rules that you helped to make."

"But I'm not gonna make no rules like that," Danny interjected, smiling wisely.

"Oh, but you won't need to." I smiled back. "The whole class will. All you'll do is abide by them. And if you don't you will *force* me to take criminal action against you, as I plan to do this recess for speaking without permission."

"Already I got a feeling I don't like this new system," Danny replied, his mouth turning down.

Good! I thought, but said instead, "Let's find out if you will. Just listen while I describe it. The classroom bank will be operated for a month by the top arithmetic student. Anyone in the room may earn this position through academic achievement in math. The banker will be changed at the end of each month, but not unless some other student has a better average in arithmetic.

"The bank will be nothing more than a notebook of class roster sheets on which each student's accumulated savings or expenditures are recorded as time permits. Usually the debiting and crediting will be accomplished during recesses or after classroom assignments have been completed. Therefore this extra time merits a banker's salary of $350 monthly."

After sufficient "Oh boys!" and "golleys!" had been murmured, I continued. "All earned academic work will be marked in dollars at the top of the paper. All you have to remember, in this classroom, is that we have no cents."

I allowed a few smiles and laughs before proceeding. "We are no longer interested in the number of wrong answers. Only the number right will be multiplied times the amount of classroom dollars I allocate for each correct answer on that particular test or extra credit paper. Is this perfectly clear?"

Upon receiving enough affirmative answers, I returned to the subject. "Classroom grades, for report card purposes, will be maintained separately in my grade book by my personal secretary. Since this pupil is working exclusively for me on my personal work, I will reserve the right to choose who it will be. The salary will amount to $250 monthly, because most of the work will be performed on the individual's own time.

"The grade book will be maintained in the following manner: At the top of each column will be written the name of the test or its contents, the date taken, and the total amount of money that it was possible to earn on that particular examination. This will provide a reference for each individual's dollar score recorded below it. Thus, any parent, pupil or myself can tell at a glance how every student did in relationship to others or a perfect test score. At the end of each nine weeks the column for every pupil will be totaled horizontally in each subject and a letter grade awarded, based upon a percentage previously selected by me. This will mean that only the test totals for each nine weeks will count for grades. Therefore, daily scores mean little separately but everything collectively."

"What's that mean?" Danny blurted out, and then immediately clapped his hands over his mouth.

I pretended to ignore his interruption and contrite gesture. "It means that much of the pressure and strain of daily work has been removed from teachers and pupils. And that you, Danny, will do some additional writing for speaking out," I added very calmly. I truly felt sorry for Danny. He was what is known as a compulsive classroom talker. But I knew that none of my pity must show. Any weakness now would affect the whole class and really not help Danny in the long run.

I came back to my original subject. "I shall *attempt* to explain how examination papers will be handled in this classroom from now onward." I looked meaningfully in Danny's direction before continuing. "A test will be corrected by exchanging papers and placing the amount of earned dollars at the top. Then the examination papers will be returned to their owners before they are again collected and scores recorded in the grade book by my personal secretary as previously described. Subsequently, the test papers will be forwarded to the banker for recording to each individual's account. Finally, all papers will be filed in a personal record folder for future use. Is this understood by all of you?"

I waited for any negative responses. Not receiving any, I offered more information on the system. "From now on, the whole class will help make classroom laws and determine the fine for violating each. We will discuss the reasons for the regulation and you will know why it is needed. It will, therefore, become everyone's law and not just mine. Thus, its enforcement will be a matter of public policy. And every infraction will be a crime against the whole class rather than just a game to outwit the teacher's authority. No longer will any of you be able to steal the class's time, or my time. You will have to pay for teacher attention in hard-earned academic money. This means that classroom 'clowns,' " again I glanced in Danny's direction, "will undoubtedly get the best education of any pupil in the room. The rascals of this room will have to study hard if they are going to support their expensive misbehavior.

"Also, there will be respect for personal and property rights of others or a civil suit may be instituted." I noticed an excessive number of incredulous expressions. "That's right! One pupil may sue another and collect his academic money if three things can be proved. First, there *must* be some damage, and this doesn't mean stepping on someone's toe accidentally. Second, there must be reliable witnesses. And third, the pupil bringing the suit must have 'clean hands.' That is, he may not have instigated the action for which he is bringing the suit—he can't punch someone in the eye and then sue because he was punched back. Is this clear?"

Heads around the room nodded affirmatively.

"Some of you may be thinking: Who cares about those old academic dollars?" I glanced around the room and noticed a few guilty smiles beginning to spread. My question, I knew then, had hit home. "But my answer to these individuals would have to be, everyone will care, just everyone. Students who allow their bank account to drop below zero are in 'bankruptcy.' "

"A bankrupt pupil loses all rights and privileges as a free citizen of this classroom and becomes a ward of the state, meaning me, just as most students are in many conventional classrooms now. The moment that any pupil goes into bankruptcy, I shall direct all of his activities until he works himself out through academic endeavor. In a manner of speaking, this individual has demonstrated his inability to control himself and must rely upon the government for direction. This will mean that even permission to leave your seat must be asked and received. Drinks during classtime will be denied, and trips to the restroom will be begged first before they are allowed. Persons in bankruptcy will be the last to leave the room at recess or dismissal time, with their free periods primarily devoted to earning academic money, rather than play. Homework will be scheduled for the bankrupt student every evening while the rest of the class will receive none."

I saw the faces of many students as they mirrored their feelings, and I knew that my words were having the desired effect. And assurance came when Danny actually raised his hand and waited for permission to speak.

"Will the academic money we lose, because of misbehavior, cause our grades to go down?"

"No, Danny, at least not in any academic subject. Only your grade in deportment and conduct will drop. Academic tests and examinations alone control the grade you will be given in subject matter, as I explained previously with the grade book."

Encouraged by Danny's effort at self-control, I moved deeper into the aspect of enforcement.

"In the past, most of your teachers have allowed you to elect a classroom president, vice-president and a secretary. This will also be accomplished in here. However, there will be some significant differences. Our president will become my right arm for the enforcement of classroom laws. In the event that I am absent from the room for any purpose, the president will act in my place. He will have my full power and authority behind him. So if he says jump, just ask 'How high?'

If you feel that the president has been unfair or has exceeded his authority, don't take the law into your own hands and defy him. Instead, do as you are told, then wait until I return. Your case, and the surrounding circumstances, will be arbitrated out of court first, and, if necessary, settled in court. Any damage you suffer will be made right. Any other course of action immediately places you in the wrong, and I shall deal with you accordingly. If your president demonstrates his inability to hold the job, he may be impeached by a two-thirds majority vote of the class and a new one elected for the remainder of that month. Therefore, don't just complain about your elected officials; do something about them."

This time Henry's hand was raised. I nodded permission in his direction. "What do you mean by the court? Who is that?"

Elated now with this additional assurance of growing pupil self-control, I offered my explanation. "For the time being, I will be the judge and jury, since I am the most impartial person in the room. When you, as a class, progress to the point of intelligence where justice can be dispensed, I will allow you to assume this duty. However, there will always be a Supreme Court, composed of one adult teacher and two students from another classroom which will hear appeals from any decision I might make. But before *any* court action is taken the facts of the case should be arbitrated out of court. The guilty party can save himself one hundred and fifty dollars in court costs if he throws himself upon the mercy of the court and settles out of court. Therefore, guilty parties should be encouraged not to waste the court's time and admit their wrongdoing, pay for the damage, and learn the lesson taught."

John sought permission to speak and I gave it. "Gee, it looks to me like this is a system of nothing but punishment and torture."

"On the contrary, John, there is no punishment except that which the pupil cares to inflict upon himself. The message is this: 'Live within the law or pay the penalty you know exists.' Your question leads us to the pleasant side of the system. I was about to explain the auction which will interest all of you.

"Once a month we will have an auction where many delightful things will be sold to the highest bidder. For instance, five seats in my automobile can be bought for a trip to the mountains, hiking, or to the seashore where the marine life will be studied. Perhaps we will go fishing, down to the zoo, or to Disneyland, if you like. The trip might be as close as the nearest bowling alley, indoor swimming pool, or skating rink."

As I proceeded to name other delightful excursions, I watched all eyes light up with enthused interest. This, I thought to myself, is the very thing missing in the environment of most children. I had long felt that it was the cause of many social problems. Few adults anywhere have the time or inclination to offer kids healthy alternatives to drugs, crime, sex, and other pseudo-thrills. Most parents who even attempt to fulfill this need drag their children up to a favorite lake time after time, not because their son or daughter likes to fish, but instead because mom or dad enjoys it. With a flash of rare insight, I saw for the first time what my pupils were probably seeing.

"We will make a list of all the different places where you would like to go and then vote for those trips you might wish to purchase at auction each month. The list will be posted on the bulletin board and academic money may be saved for the time it will be sold."

I decided that there was no time like the present to put my suggestion into action. After much discussion and many proposals by the class, the youngsters voted for nine journeys that I secretly wanted them to take. Naturally, it required some salesmanship on my part to convince them that these particular trips were the best. During the process of persuasion, I exercised great care to conceal my maneuverings, since to have done otherwise would have destroyed the very motivation that I was attempting to accomplish. After the tantalizing list had been posted, I continued with further auction time explanations.

"There will be many other exciting items sold at auction. As an example, the highest bidder may purchase the right to become king or queen for any selected day during the succeeding month. The king or queen may advise me regarding the subjects to be taught for that specific day. "Naturally," I grinned at the class, "I expect his majesty to wait for an especially heavy test day before mounting his throne and issuing suggestions."

On the other hand, I thought to myself, pupils should also expect me merely to give these same examinations on the following day. But fortunately for me, perhaps, children wouldn't think this clearly, and the day's hero would still remain just that.

"Another enticing item sold at auction is the right to move your seat. In the past, most teachers have not permitted you to sit where you please, because you talk too much to your friends. This will not become a problem under our new system. Fines will soon convince you that sitting next to a friend can be costly indeed. And speaking of fines, I believe that we have reached a time for their implementation."

There was a lively discussion after each classroom law was proposed by either a pupil or myself. Strangely, students, given the opportunity, were much harsher on themselves than their teacher would have been. In fact, I was hard put to temper fines and guide votes in the proper direction. At last, the job was completed to my satisfaction. I realized that I had sneakily used my adult dictatorial powers, but also knew that I had no other choice until my pupils could perform these governmental functions intelligently themselves.

One innovation to come out of this legislative session was the card system for classroom conversation. My pupils decided that everyone should be allowed to talk in whispers. But no one, including myself, could offer any acceptable criterion for a whisper. So I was made the judge of this weighty question. If I felt that the pupil was talking too loud, I would merely say, "Ears, John!" or "Ears, Susie!" The statement meant that the offending student would have to cup both hands around a listener's ear whenever he spoke for the rest of that day.

The following fines were voted for talking violations: First offense, ten dollars; the second, twenty dollars; and all subsequent infractions, $100 each. A new day would wipe the offender's slate clean, and future penalty adjustments were at my discretion.

The card system evolved from a tangible need to know. Something had to be visible to remind classroom conversationalists of the rights they enjoyed at a specific moment. About this time, Mr. Turner poked his head in the doorway to ask if we had any problems, and then managed to suggest a color scheme for identification before leaving.

So it was decided that colored cards would be displayed on the chalk tray. A red card would mean no talking at all, the yellow card glued students to their seats until permission to move was received, and the green card indicated a right to whisper. Two cards could be displayed at the same time except for red and green, and individual pupils could be put on red or yellow by the teacher. The classroom president was to use a class roster called the fine sheet to record each infraction as directed by the teacher, and this fine sheet would be given to the banker at the end of each day for debiting to individual accounts. The previous decisions consumed all of thirty minutes and we paused in our efforts only long enough to elect a president, vice president, and secretary.

Finally, with our classroom laws voted and posted, I picked up the outline of the system which I had devised the night before. What was the next item to be covered? At this moment the recess bell rang. I was gratified to see that no pupil ran for the door. They all sat in their seat and looked expectantly in my direction. Boy O boy! I thought, the system *is* working.

"Everyone but Danny may go out to play."

Again I was amazed to see my pupils depart as young ladies and gentlemen instead of animals. Danny sat with his elbows propped on his desk and his head cradled in his hands.

"Danny! Go over to the book shelf by the window and get a dictionary. Turn to page twenty-three and copy all of the words and their first meaning. When you're finished, give it to me."

While Danny complied, I lost myself in a review of the morning's developments. Some aspects of the new system seemed to be working even better than I had hoped. If what I still had to cover was only half as successful, the program would be great. Self-reliance for my pupils wasn't nearly as far away as I thought. The ringing school bell broke into my thoughts, signaling the end of the recess.

Pupils calmly entered the classroom and sat in their seats without saying a word. Perspiration glistened on most foreheads and many fanned themselves with whatever came handy. The silence in the classroom was almost eerie until I happened to glance at the chalk tray. The green card had fallen off and the red card glared its warning. I got up, walked over, and placed the green card in front of the red. A very light murmur washed over the room as conversations began. I felt like dancing but contented myself with a comment.

"See, class! Isn't this great? Now we can make progress with anything we care to do. And you will find that the longer you use this new system the more you will like it."

Susie's hand went up from the back of the room, and I offered permission.

"Will we use play money, Mr. Harrison?"

"Yes," I replied, "as soon as I can get it dittoed. This will make our economy more like real life. However, cash is not necessary to make our system work."

I walked back to my desk, picked up a typed sheet of paper and waved it at the class. "This contains a list of 'classroom companies' with a description of the functions for each, together with earning potentials. The license, to operate each one for a month, will be sold at auction. Please let me name just a few. Anyone may purchase the 'Pencil Company.' This organization rents pencils for ten dollars daily or sells them for $150. All profit becomes the property of the owner, just as any loss must be assumed in the same way. As a miniature business-man, the company is your baby to rock as you choose."

This solicited some smiles, but of more importance, their attention was sharpened. It seemed to me that everyone's curiosity was aroused.

"Another popular enterprise should be the 'Bathroom Company.' This young entrepreneur will schedule his classmates to the restroom at ten dollars a trip during classtime, unless the individual is sick. At recess time it's free, as it is with all of the companies. In the future, the 'Water Company' will sell drinks at five dollars apiece and the 'Book Company' may rent textbooks to any pupil who forgets his. There will be a 'Clean Up Company' to inspect untidy desks and dirty areas, and also a 'Service Company' will exist to operate our audio-visual equipment and to pick a different *teacher's pet* daily."

I observed the growing excitement with secret delight. Most kids want, and need, to become doers and not just watchers and listeners in a dictatorship.

"We will have a 'Finance Company,' an 'Information Company,' and a 'Supply Company,' as well as many more. In fact, we are not much more limited in our choices than your parents are in real life.

"In addition to the commercial type of company, there will be 'academic companies,' such as the 'Spelling,' 'Arithmetic,' and 'Vocab-ulary Companies.' The purpose of each of these will be to promote skills, knowledge, and speed in that specific subject."

The amazement of most students, by now, was genuine and a pleas-ure to watch. This seemed an appropriate moment to spring my final bombshell for the day. I knew that the class had received about all that it could effectively absorb for now. Other planned innovations would have to await their turn for an appropriate introduction. Per-haps I was making a mistake to add even this bombshell, since it did involve a vast concept. But after only a moment's thought, I decided to risk it. The tremendous good its immediate presentation could achieve far outweighed any other consideration.

"Now, boys and girls, I am going to describe a portion of our new program which possibly provides more valuable contributions to education than everything previously presented. This new technique is really not new. It was used as long ago as the little one room school-house, but I have merely added a new twist. The method offers fan-tastic academic achievement opportunities for all of you through instant aid to the slow learner and it also gives leadership training to the talented. Probably for the first time, pupils will be unchained from a lockstep type of education. So you can see why all of you must listen carefully to my description and explanation."

I paused to survey the class reaction only to discover that my last statement was wholly unnecessary. All eyeballs were focused on me and even many mouths were ajar.

"Every student in this classroom is eligible to earn a 'Teachership' in our major academic subjects. The top fifth of the class will become student teachers and receive the privilege of selecting their own five pupils from among the remaining classmates. Each student teacher will earn one-fifth of whatever his pupils earn at test time, in addition to his own earnings on the test. This means that pupils who are not learning will reduce that teacher's earning power. Therefore, student teachers will not only want to help their pupils to learn but will probably devise ways to see that they do. So you can see that the way to riches in this room is through academic effort and that the means to achieve it are readily available to everyone."

John's hand waving in the air at the back of the room caught my eye. "Yes, John, what is it?"

"It's five minutes after twelve and lunch period has started. I guess the office must have forgot to ring the bell."

I turned around and quickly glanced at the overhead clock on the wall. "So it is. All right, you are dismissed, but remember to act like young ladies and gentlemen. Our classroom laws have the longest arm you have ever seen. They easily reach to the playground and even apply to riding the bus in the morning or at night." I waved my hand toward the door to indicate that they were dismissed.

CHAPTER 5

Afternoon of the Second Day
The System in Operation Within the Classroom

The coolness of the closed classroom bathed our sweaty bodies as I opened the door at 1 p.m., but this refreshing atmosphere was only momentary. Thirty-five perspiring dynamos demanded that all windows and doors be opened immediately to the tender mercy of the 107-degree California sun.

The major portion of my lunch hour had been spent dittoing our classroom "funny money." I had fives, tens, twenties, fifties and hundreds tucked under my arm. Naturally, this caused a stir of excitement and curiosity. The chatter and questions grew by the seconds. I finished stacking the bills in an old fishing tackle box that I had brought for the purpose and then snapped the padlock before walking to the chalk tray to turn the green talking card to red.

The resulting silence made my day. Even Danny went through the pretended though unnecessary motions of warning his colleagues. Incredible, I thought. This is as a classroom should be. Perhaps children can learn other responsibilities and disciplines besides just academic.

My voice seemed loud, yet I knew I was speaking softly. "I spent over two hours last evening in a review of your personnel records for the purpose of selecting a few classroom officers. Next month, each of you will have the opportunity of selecting yourself since these positions will be earned through weekly tests that you take."

"The classroom banker will be Jim Mowery, due to his past demonstrated abilities in the field of mathematics and other social characteristics desirable for the job."

I handed Jim the locked cash box, with a key, before continuing. "Jim will maintain a class roster sheet called the 'bank sheet,' on which will be recorded all deposits, whether from academic earnings or business transactions, and withdrawals will be reflected similarly."

I paused to survey the reception of this information. Failing to find any perplexed faces, I returned to my subject. "The bank will be open for cash withdrawals or deposits only ten minutes in the morning and again ten minutes just before you are dismissed for the day. Also, at the banker's convenience during recess, if a ten dollar per customer service charge is paid to the banker. Any questions?"

Danny's hand shot into the air. Pleased with his apparent self-control, I gave permission immediately.

"Suppose all thirty-five of us want to put our money in, or take our money out of the bank the same morning? How can we do this in ten minutes?"

"Easy!" I replied. "A deposit or withdrawal slip will be completed and placed beforehand in the correct box provided for that purpose. Thus, the banker can make his bookkeeping entry prior to the ten minute opening time and then use the ten minute period almost exclusively for the collection or disbursement of cash."

I noticed John's hand waving frantically at the back of the room. I nodded permission.

"What happens if I run out of cash during the day?"

"Well," I said with a twinkle in my eye, "Who can tell me what happens in real life when this occurs?"

"You can't buy nothing!" Danny shouted and then clapped his hands over his mouth with all the contriteness of which he was capable.

I smiled despite myself. At least he was starting to recognize his errors and responsibilities. Danny's improvement called for praise; nevertheless, the penalty couldn't be overlooked.

"I'm sorry, Danny," I said sadly, "but you stole the opportunity of the class to answer. In accordance with our voted classroom laws, you are fined ten dollars for your first offense today. Also, inasmuch as you don't have any cash I am forced to double the amount you would ordinarily pay. This added cost is called a carrying charge in the adult business world and is in the nature of interest on a loan."

I pointed toward my desk and then nodded in the direction of our recently elected classroom president. "Frank! Please get a class roster sheet and label it 'Fine Sheet.' Now mark twenty dollars in a circle below Danny's name. The Fine Sheet should be handed to the banker daily for subtraction from individual accounts.

"Now, to get back to John's original question. Has this little demonstration with Danny solved the problem of what happens if you don't have any cash?"

I waited for John to nod his assent before proceeding. "Jim, will you please credit $500 to everyone's account and then pass out withdrawal slips to any pupil wishing cash. After this, all classroom debts will be paid with 'Harrison dollars' or else the amount owed will be doubled due to the carrying charge. And another thing, please remember that bankrupt pupils have no purchasing power during classtime since they have neither cash nor good credit."

I noticed, with much pleasure, Danny's hand waving frantically in the back of the room. I nodded immediate permission.

"I guess I'll probably be the first one broke and won't have no ten dollars to pay the bathroom company. Does this mean that I'll have to pee on the floor?"

Naturally, this put the class into an uproar and I smiled in spite of myself. "No, Danny! *True* welfare cases can petition the state to receive a 'Welfare Pass,' so students never need to *wet* their pants. And I wish to make this very clear: Any pupil who has a medical problem requiring extra restroom time or drinking water should see me privately. In some cases a permanent pass will be given just as government assistance is offered in real life to the blind, helpless and those truly deserving.

"Believe it or not," my voice unconsciously lifted with enthusiasm, "most answers to your questions about our new system can be found by using real life as a pattern, and it is here that you should search first. From now on you will learn that you must pay for your mistakes and that daily responsibilities meaningful to your age group must be shouldered.

"Perhaps some of you thought that Danny was treated unfairly when he had to pay carrying charges without first having the opportunity to acquire cash."

I ignored Danny's head nodding vigorously at the back of the room and continued. "If you did, let me point out that life itself can sometimes be unfair; therefore, the lesson should be learned early. For instance, it's not fair that some people are constantly sick while others are always healthy, or that some couples can have many children and others none. It just happened to be Danny's unlucky lot to have spoken before any cash could be dispensed. But after all, he did violate the law he helped to make and therefore must pay the penalty prescribed."

Danny, as well as most of the class, appeared to understand what

I had said so I thought it might be safe to let the subject die. At least it was fortunate, I felt, that our new system permitted the youngsters to experience unfairness inside the classroom rather than as adults.

I walked casually over to the chalkboard and began writing the names and titles of newly elected officers in the upper left corner. In the upper right hand corner I wrote the name of each business and its newly-selected owner. As I printed I reminded students that all businesses are merely leased from month to month. Each company lease would be sold to the highest bidder at auction time henceforth.

I returned to my desk and opened the teacher's edition for mathematics.

"Students! Please open your arithmetic book and be certain that your name is written inside the front cover. Next, turn to the inside back cover and write the following: 'My student teacher is·········· ················.'"

I walked up and down the aisles to insure compliance before divulging the names of the five most competent math pupils.

"The student teachers just named will go outside now and select their pupils from the remainder of the class. Please use a class roster sheet to X the people selected and then cross out those picked by another student teacher. While teachers are picking pupils the rest of the class will accomplish the test on page twenty-eight. Please begin now."

I stood in the doorway where I could observe both the teachers and my pupils as they carried out instructions. Amazingly, the student teachers accomplished their task with very little confusion or additional instruction. In less than fifteen minutes the teachers returned to the room with their results. I directed them to stand at the rear of each of the five rows of desks where they read the names of their pupils. As a name was called, that pupil copied his or her student teacher's name in the blank space previously provided on the inside back cover of the math textbook.

"All pupils," I announced, "will now move into their proper row and sit as directed by your student teacher. Please do this as rapidly as possible and keep the talking at a minimum."

The first part of my last sentence was a mistake and the remainder went unheard. Some of my speedsters vaulted desks and, in general, most acted like animals in their efforts to find a choice seat.

"Freeze!" I bellowed. "The first one to move will pay a fifty-dollar fine."

The results now were almost worth the previous confusion and chaos. Muscles quivered and bodies swayed, but basically everyone stayed completely immobile.

"All right!" I forced myself to become calm once again. "After I release you—I haven't said you were released yet, so get that leg back up there, Danny," I speared the chubby culprit with an angry eye, and he immediately complied.

"As I was saying, when you're released I'll give you two minutes to get properly seated in your correct row. Anyone found out of his seat beyond this time limit will pay a fifty-dollar fine. And any running or jockeying for positions will be considered playing in the classroom which brings a fifty-dollar 'diaper' fine. Your time starts from *now*."

I divided my attention between the class and my watch. There was time to spare and my pupils' deportment would have warmed the heart of my old Air Force drill instructor.

"From now on," I said with all the firmness I could muster, "everyone will move into whatever academic group I name in exactly this same manner within a ninety-second time limit or suffer a fifty-dollar fine."

I cringed inwardly with the realization that my high-handed actions smacked of despotism rather than the self-reliant principles I initially desired to teach. But I also realized that, for the present, common sense demanded no other course. Until my pupils could be trained to live as humans they would require treatment as animals. The whole class moved through two more practices before I was satisfied.

I followed these same procedures for each of the remaining five major subjects. Student teachers were named, and they selected pupils. Groups were entered and tests completed. The whole thing became sufficiently routine to insure future orderliness. The school day departed almost before I knew it and everyone became so enthused that many students begged for overtime when the dismissal bell rang.

CHAPTER 6
Morning of the Third Day
Doctoring the Sores

My pupils opened the day with the pledge of allegiance and then a class-selected song. Surprisingly, my nervous tension was gone. This was a great joy since it permitted me to ponder the problems and analyze some remedies. As we sang, I tried to recall some of the weaknesses that arose my first day. Immediately, Henry's cheating came to mind. Here was a classroom evil that plagued most instructors. Any improvement our new system could achieve in this area would certainly be welcome.

I would allow my pupils to exchange yesterday's examination papers. I could learn much just from observing what would happen. I handed the stack of math tests to the owner of the Service Company with the following instructions: "Please pass these out and make sure that no one gets his own paper. Also give a boy's paper to a girl and a girl's to a boy, and try to keep friends from checking each other's test.

"Say, Luke! You must have forgotten to read the dittoed instructions on running the businesses. Please select a different teacher's pet daily and place the name in the upper left hand corner of the chalkboard. Would you do this now, please?"

I observed, with satisfaction, that most pupils had written, or were writing, "Checked by" and their names at the bottom of papers. I felt duty-bound to issue a final warning.

"Please put 'Checked by' and your name at the bottom of the paper. This will be the last time I warn you. In the future twenty-five dollars will be paid to the owner of the paper by the checker in every case of negligence. Also, any mischecking of an answer costs a dollar each. Therefore, if you don't understand an answer or can't hear it whenever it's read, you'd better hold up your hand for a repeat. From now on shiftlessness or laziness in this room will be costly."

I handed the new teacher's pet my teacher's edition for math. "Here, Larry! Please read the answers slowly. Give your paper to someone else to check."

I turned to address the whole class. "And there better be no cheating. Just remember the $200 fine if you're caught. But if that doesn't deter you, here is another thought that should. It is no longer possible to cheat the teacher; instead the thief will be picking the pocket of friends. When auction time arrives everything is sold to the highest bidder. This means that the cheater can accumulate enough dishonest funds to outbid his trustworthy neighbor. Therefore, it is each student's civic duty to report any dishonest behavior of colleagues. No longer will anyone be considered a tattletale who reports infractions of our classroom laws. In fact, you can be charged as an accessory if you don't."

I watched the checking process as it proceeded, well aware of the need for vigilance. My thoughts turned toward the conventional elementary classroom where the harassed teacher seldom has time for the incessant complainer and tattler who, in her mind, enjoys troublemaking just for the sport of it. Therefore, pupils learn early to mind their own business and not become involved. This has developed a nation of civic-minded citizens who frequently manage to look the other way when a robbery, rape or even murder occurs right under their nose. The cry of this righteous soul is: "I just can't afford to become involved in that!" So the crime rate soars.

A waving hand from the back of the room attracted my attention and broke my reverie.

"Yes, Marie! What is it?"

"Bill is cheating. I saw him change two answers on John's paper, both seven and eleven.

"Bring the paper you are correcting to me, please, Bill," I asked, and he complied. After an examination of the clumsily erased and changed answers, I put the question to Bill. "Well, *did* you change these?"

The positive reply was plain to read in Bill's features, but there was something more—a sullenness that seemed to question my right to ask.

"Yeh! So what?" Bill growled and then fixed his eyes on the classroom floor. "This is nothing but a silly game you got us playing in here, and even my dad thinks so."

I felt my anger rise and the color drain from my face, but I tried hard not to show it in my reply. "Perhaps you and your father are right, Bill, but isn't life itself exactly the same type of game in which we must learn to abide by rules or laws until we can change them?"

Without waiting for Bill's reply, I continued. "Therefore, in accordance with our classroom laws, please pay me $200 for cheating."

Bill's eyes came up from the floor to fix on mine, with defiance shining forth. "All I've got is a hundred dollar bill so I guess you'll have to accept that." His hand held out the bill and I took it.

"I'm sorry, Bill, but you'll have to guess again." My voice was sympathetic and I made myself ignore his obvious sneering attitude. "You still owe the state $100 and with the carrying charge it comes to a total of $200."

I turned to the banker before issuing my instructions. "Please deduct $200 from Bill's account."

My gaze swung back to Bill's face which was now contorted with rage. He reached into his pocket and pulled out two more hundred dollar bills which he threw in my direction.

"You can take all of your damn money and stick it," he cried, tears streaming down his face. "I'm not going to play your silly game no more." So saying, he flung himself back into his seat.

"And that display of rudeness and disrespect," I said, fighting to stay calm, "will cost you an additional $300 fine."

I then told the banker to pick up the money from the floor and also deduct the additional amount from Bill's bank account. Next, I returned my attention to Bill. "Did you really mean what you said about dropping out of our new classroom system?"

I waited for Bill to nod his assent before continuing. "All right, Bill! You or any other pupil, at this time only, may drop out of the system. Let's see a show of hands of those desiring to do so."

It was gratifying to observe only three hands waving in the air. "Before I can permit you to do this, an explanation is in order. This opportunity is only available now. At no later date will dropping be tolerated, no matter how far into debt you may go or how much you want out. Our new system is patterned after life, which means that any bed you make you must occupy. And this is as it should be. Responsibilities should never be shirked merely as the whim or fancy hits us. However, inasmuch as you have not yet had an opportunity, in this room, to acquire any responsibilities, you do have a choice. But please remember this: Anyone outside of the system will be required to work and produce at exactly the same rate without pay other than the personal reward of a job well done. Further, those outside of the system will have very little self-control and even less opportunity to exercise it. On the other hand, the outsider will also have less responsibility and suffer fewer losses since he will have so little to lose. As your teacher and classroom director, I will furnish whatever I think you need. Your choice, as I see it, is this: you may either work for something more or for something less. Now, once again I will ask, how many want to be outside of the system?"

Only one hand raised, Bill's.

"Very well, Bill. From now on you are like the man without a country who was forced to continuously sail the seas without ever setting foot ashore."

I related some of the details concerning this hapless fellow who renounced his country. I finished my tale with this happy thought. "However, unlike this poor man, you, Bill, will be allowed to re-enter our system whenever you are willing to make the move on a permanent basis."

Bill, still sulking, pretended to ignore my offer and sank still deeper into his seat. After this, everything seemed to progress smoothly. We finished checking most of the tests by the time the recess bell rang. The class filed out of the room in an orderly manner. I sat down, cocked my feet up on the desk, and put my hands behind my head— a favorite daydreaming position.

After three days in the classroom I certainly couldn't be considered an authority on child psychology, this I knew. But if my school children were any guide it seemed to me that educational institutions were sadly remiss in not teaching the practical aspects of living. Hopefully, as time passed, I could discover new ways to use our innovative system as a remedy.

But of more immediate need was a cure for the atrocious grammar sprayed at me all day long. Perhaps we could start a fine for every offender. Suddenly, the solution was there. Why not have a Bingo program? The details gradually began to form in my mind, but the bell rang before I had everything complete.

Determined to experiment with my new-found technique, I decided to start Bingo right away. I turned the card on red, with the usual warning about silence. The room became quiet immediately, and then I flipped the card back to green.

"We are going to play Bingo in this room." An excited whisper of curiosity washed across the room.

"Easy on the talking," I admonished, "or you will force me to turn the card on red.

"Now, as I was saying, Bingo will give the sharp grammar student, who also listens well, a chance to make some extra money. From tomorrow onward, any pupil who hears another use incorrect grammar, and has a witness, will receive five dollars from the incorrect speaker, if he softly says 'Bingo' and then provides the proper grammatical correction. However, no one will collect on any grammatical error that has not been first taught to the whole class by me. This will prevent confusion as to what is or is not correct. Also, it gives everyone an equal opportunity to collect a Bingo from his neighbor.

"Is there anyone who does not understand what I have said so far?" I paused and looked around the room.

Failing to receive any response to my question, I proceeded. "All right! This is the proper procedure to follow when someone Bingos on another: First, say Bingo very softly, since the loud talker is still subject to the classroom fine. Second, tell the person what he said wrong and then correct the sentence grammatically. Third, the corrected pupil must give his Bingoer an IOU for five dollars which, at the correcter's convenience, is signed on the back and then placed in the Bingo Box kept by the number-one student language teacher. When the language teacher finds time, he will review all IOUs for proper debiting and crediting. This will be accomplished on a class roster sheet labeled Bingo Sheet at the top. At the end of each week the Bingo Sheet will be totaled by the language teacher and then handed to the banker for recording in bank accounts. Also, at this time the number-two language teacher will assume the duty for the following week.

"Are the details of what I just said clear to everyone?" I waited for a response until Susie timidly raised her hand.

"Suppose neither the witness nor the one you Bingo on believes that the sentence is really wrong?"

"All disputes will first be taken to the language teacher. If he deems it necessary he will then bring it to my attention for a final settlement."

Danny's hand shot up from the back of the room and I nodded permission.

"Can I even Bingo on you and collect five dollars if you don't talk right?" Danny's mischievous smile made his whole face light up.

"Yes, Danny, you may. And there will be many times when I purposely make grammatical errors just to see which pupils are on their toes." And, I thought to myself, there will also be many times when their stupid teacher can cover real mistakes with this little maneuver and not appear the complete jackass. "Also, Danny, what do you mean by talk right? If you mean enunciation or pronunciation errors, no one will be allowed to Bingo on these. And I might also add that some of you would-be clowns will not be permitted to purposely disturb the class with Bingos. This could be considered playing in the classroom and rate a fifty dollar diaper fine."

John raised his hand and I offered permission. "Suppose two or more people Bingo at the same time?"

"Then the state gets the IOU." I was losing too much time and needed to proceed. "If there are no more questions, let's move to another subject. Tomorrow most Bingo problems will be solved as we use it."

I asked the class to move into their reading groups which they did, promptly and without excessive noise. Evidently our previous drill had paid off.

"Before we actually begin work," I said, "it will be necessary to cover some basic material which you should have learned in lower grades but probably didn't."

A hand popped up from the far left corner which I recognized with a tilt of my head.

"Mr. Harrison! Somebody stole all my cash. I left it in my desk and when I came back from the bathroom it was gone." Henry's face seemed even grayer than normal.

I surveyed the room. "Is there anyone in here who knows anything about this?"

"I saw Henry put his money in his desk," Ray volunteered, "but I never saw nobody take it out."

"Well, Henry!" I said, trying to ease the hurt, "I guess you have learned a cheap lesson. After all it could have been a real hundred dollar bill. And, although it may be hard for you to believe now, it's really a blessing in disguise. This merely means that you're going to have to work a little harder academically to earn it back and in the process you will get a little better education."

"Yeh, man! You can say that," Henry shook his head sadly, "since you ain't the one that has to work and earn it."

I gave him a sympathy smile. "Perhaps you're right, Henry. However everyone should learn a lesson from this—we have a classroom need here. Who knows what it is?"

Ray raised his hand and I recognized him. "Something has to be done about thieves. Somebody swiped fifty dollars from me yesterday."

"You're right!" I replied. "But what would you suggest?"

"How about a police force and I'll be the chief?" Ray countered.

"This is certainly one alternative," I offered. "But let's look to the adult world in which we live for the best answer. Police would certainly help. However, is something available that might prevent the theft in the first place?"

John's hand raised. I nodded. "How about writing checks instead of using cash? Or maybe we could buy money orders or travelers checks."

"Beautiful, John! That's real thinking," I complimented. "I think you should be entitled to operate the Check Company until we sell it at auction. Get a ditto master and make up a sheet for the Ditto Company to run off. Allow anyone to buy checks at the rate of five dollars for each $100 written. For instance, $525 would be deposited with you and entitle that person to write up to $500 in checks. Anyone overdrawn must pay the customary carrying charge of double the cash amount to you."

Naturally, the thought of writing checks and transacting business just like their fathers and mothers caused excited whispers to become louder and louder. I walked over, turned the card to red, and made the required announcement of that fact. When the room was silent I turned the card back to green.

"We have spent enough time on new operational details," I stated. "Let's review some of the tools used in reading. Who can correctly say the short vowels?"

Not many hands raised, which came as no shock.

"I'm going to sound each short vowel," I said. "Everybody say it after me. As soon as everyone here knows them we'll play a new type of game."

I spent about fifteen minutes in a review before pairing students inside each group. One pupil listened while the other spelled, rather than read, the words in sentences from the California Reading Textbook. Whenever a vowel was encountered it was pronounced the short way rather than with the long sound as is customary. Students were timed. At the end of one minute, vowels were counted and earned one dollar for two. Any mistake during the timed period, as judged by the listener, stopped the contestant and he could count only the vowels up to that point.

Excitement ran high. It was unbelievable. Students wanted to continue beyond the lunch bell and it was only with my firm insistence that they left for the cafeteria. After my pupils had gone I sat down at my desk to collect my thoughts for a moment. This vowel game seemed the perfect way to reading improvement. Hopefully, my pupils could soon progress beyond just short vowels and say each letter, or combination thereof, exactly the way it sounded in the word.

The knocking at the door broke the spell and I asked whoever it was to enter.

Susie poked her head inside, her voice excited and urgent. "Bill and Henry are causing trouble in the lunch line!"

I got up, locked the door and followed Susie to the cafeteria. Bill and Henry were seated on a bench by themselves. First I checked with the school cashier and then consulted with the class President, Frank. They confirmed Susie's warning. Both boys had been disorderly and had caused a disturbance. I motioned Bill to me.

"Go to the office and report exactly what happened to the principal. Afterward, I want you to describe to me what punishment you received." I waved him away and beckoned for Henry.

"Of course, Henry, you realize that this must be considered as embarrassing the class, which brings a $200 fine."

I waited for Henry to indicate that he understood. He reached into his pocket and paid me with two hundred-dollar bills.

"All right, Henry. You may rejoin the lunch line."

I called Frank to me. "I hope you understand that in my absence you are in charge of the class and responsible for its proper behavior. In the future, first warn students and then fine them in my name. If they give you any trouble about this, remind them that they can always take you to court if they think you are wrong or unfair, just as they can me."

CHAPTER 7
Afternoon of the Third Day
Developing Additional Techniques

The bell rang, ending the lunch recess. I opened the classroom door and my pupils filed inside. What a pleasing change from the first day, I thought. However, it was apparent from the attitudes and behavior I saw that some great catastrophe had occurred on the playground. I waited until all were seated before broaching the subject.

"Well, what happened?" I questioned.

The room exploded, with every pupil trying to explain at once. I rushed over to the chalk tray, turned the card on red, and warned the class that I had done so. The results were beautiful. Just like turning the volume knob on a radio. If the system did nothing else, it was worth any amount of trouble for this kind of classroom control.

"Now, hands up and I'll call on you individually," I said. Arms were raised all over the room. I chose Danny since he displayed a big lump over his eye and obviously had a tale to tell about something.

"I'm gonna sue Henry. He smashed me in the eye."

"He called me a nigger again!" Henry snarled, his face sweaty and angry.

"Calm down, Henry!" I admonished, my palms waving toward him. "You should know that I would call on you next. But now that outburst will cost you ten dollars." My hand stretched toward him for collection.

Reluctantly he dug into his pocket for the required money and handed it over with a scowl.

I thanked Henry and turned to Danny. "Okay! Tell your side of it first and then Henry can tell his."

Substantially, the situation was much as I surmised. Henry was monopolizing the swings again and Danny swung the only weapon he knew that could hurt Henry—the words "dirty nigger!" Thereupon, Henry, according to Henry, gave Danny a "love tap" in the eye.

I waited for both to finish their story before making any observations. "As I see it neither of your hands are clean. Therefore, it boils down to a case for damages. Danny's injury is physical and Henry's mental. The difference might come to fifty dollars in favor of Danny, if both of you are willing to settle out of court for this amount."

"But I want more than that!" Danny demanded.

"I'm certain that you do, Danny," I replied. "And it's your right to go into court tomorrow, during one of the recesses. But if all of the facts are brought out, you might just lose the case, and have to pay the $150 in court costs. Also, the other two judges might not feel that you rate any more damages than I do, which would mean that you had wasted your time."

"All right!" Danny said with resignation. "I'll accept fifty dollars."

"How about you, Henry?" I asked.

"Ya!" Henry grunted, obviously pleased to get out this cheaply. "It's worth fifty any day to pound Danny. The only trouble is I don't have no more money."

"Not even in your bank account?" I asked, surprised.

Henry shook his head negatively, "I drew it all out in cash."

"Well, what do you know?" I said still surprised. "I guess we have our first bankruptee."

I turned to Jim, the banker, and directed him to deduct the fifty dollars for Danny and fifty dollars for the carrying charge. Henry's name was to be posted prominently on the chalkboard for all businessmen to see and be warned accordingly. Also, the Bankruptcy Company took charge of Henry's homework, recesses and privileges, as he was now a "state ward."

I sensed that we had spent sufficient time in non-academic areas. We needed to get back on the subject matter trail. However, I was secretly very pleased. My class had learned much this afternoon in the business of everyday living. And what an improvement over the last time we had a playground fracas!

"Please return to your reading-group seats and we will work on comprehension," I requested. "Take paper, pencil and social studies textbook with you."

The transfer from home seats to group seats was made in an orderly manner within the required ninety-second time limit. I spent approximately twenty minutes in a discussion of topic sentences before instructing my student teachers to help their pupils find topic sentences in the state social studies textbook.

After ten minutes of practice, I issued the following instructions. "Everyone please turn to page thirty-two. When I say start, you will have fifteen minutes to either locate or compose as many topic sentences from the paragraphs on this page as you can. Each correct topic sentence will pay five dollars. Teachers may help their pupils in an advisory capacity only. Under no circumstances will a teacher actually do a pupil's work while in the group. I feel that more learning takes place through experience, so let the pupil do it and the teacher act as a consultant. And remember, teachers get one-fifth of their pupils' production as a bonus. So no production, no bonus. All right! Begin now!"

Again excitement ran high and the class begged for an extension of time when I made them stop. Here, I thought, was education at its best. Pupils were eager to become involved and leadership training could progress side by side with academic assistance at the moment it was needed the most.

We spent twenty minutes in correction and discussion of papers. "Student teachers," I declared, "should write down the names of their pupils, what each earned, and then divide the total by five. This sheet of calculations, together with your name and group number, should be handed to me today. Tomorrow I'll pass it on to the banker for crediting to individual accounts."

Next, the class was instructed to move into arithmetic groups and substantially the same procedure was followed. Class instruction was given, group work by student teachers was permitted, and finally a timed speed test was taken by all. Two dollars was paid for each correct answer. At this time I wisely announced that from now on I would never reveal how much each correct answer would be worth until after any test was taken. Occasionally, I told them, they would be working just for the practice and skill necessary for perfection.

As my pupils worked on arithmetic basics I felt that I could almost see their speed increase. But what was of perhaps more value, there was that certain gleam in their eyes which told me motivation was there at last. They were learning that basics could be fun rather than the dry drudgery of the conventional classroom. And when it came time to quit, they demanded more until I mentioned that most students had now accumulated sufficient money to have a quickie auction. Only a few items would be sold now, I advised, the rest would have to await our big monthly auction at the end of two weeks.

As the amount of each account was read by the banker and copied down by the respective student involved, I mulled over in my mind some of the hidden benefits I had found by using the system. No longer did pupils constantly steal class time or my time by asking me for unnecessary drinks or restroom trips. Lost pencils or erasers were bought with hard academic money. And discipline problems were no longer problems. To be sure, I had pangs as I consistently extracted money for every infraction. But every dollar spent meant that this particular rascal would have to earn it back academically and thereby get an extra education. What parent could validly object to the disciplining of his child by such a method, I thought, especially when the child was frequently the weakest academically in the class? Viewed in this light, most teachers should no longer fear discipline problems but rather welcome them as an additional opportunity to educate pupils not only in academic subjects but also in the realization that they must shoulder the responsibility for their antisocial acts. Neither mama and papa, nor the teacher would be required to pay emotionally for the student's errors. Instead, the pupil would find that he could really hurt only himself. And this realization would come not next year, not as an adult, nor when he couldn't care less, but instead, right then, when he thought it mattered the most. Classroom training of this type was sorely needed today, I was certain.

My thoughts were cut short by Banker Jim's hand waving at me. I nodded.

"We're ready for the auction now, Mr. Harrison!"

"Thank you!" I replied and picked up the list of auctionable items I had made last evening. As I studied the contents, a few basic thoughts came to me.

The auction held the real key to success of our new system. Pupils had to value the academic dollars and had to hate to lose them. The system was no more simple or complicated than that. It was up to me, as the teacher and operator of the system, to supply rewards geared to the wants or needs of ten-, eleven-, and twelve-year old boys and girls.

Personally, I don't care for bowling, but I imagined that most of my pupils would, so this was the first thing to be sold. After all, I was sure that I would never miss the two hours time nor the dollar that it would require. And who knows? Maybe I might eventually learn to enjoy bowling.

"First of all," I said, "you will need some instructions for the auction. Everything will be sold to the highest bidder. There will be *no shouting* of bids. Either say your bid softly or you may nod your head if you bid the figure I am asking. Now I realize that you are bound to become excited but if you get too loud I'll turn the card on red and then everyone will sit in silence, making a bid only by a raising of the hand.

"Also, once I accept your bid it is binding on your bank account. If you overbid the total of your cash and bank balance, you will pay the carrying charge on the balance and you will be considered bankrupt. This will result in my re-auctioning the last item you bought with a service charge for me of one-fourth of whatever it brings. Therefore, my message is this: *Don't overbid!*"

I turned to Banker Jim for my final bit of instruction. "Get a class roster sheet and label it 'Auction' at the top. Please record each bid that I accept beside that person's name. Then students can settle up with you after we have finished.

"Okay!" I exclaimed. "Here we go! I have four seats in my car to sell. The trip will be to the local bowling alley for one hour next Thursday, right after school. Each student pays for his own bowling, and I'll provide the supervision and transportation. This trip requires a note of permission from your parents at the time we go. If you don't go at the time we leave, there are no refunds.

"What am I bid for the first seat? I have a hundred dollars—two hundred—three—four. Going once, twice, and sold to Banker Jim for four hundred dollars."

I sold the remaining three seats first and then the remaining items followed in the order of their desirability. This pulled top academic dollar for each.

Two academic projects were eagerly bought. One consisted of a report on the planets and the other a written project on the Aztec Indians of Mexico. The technique here was beautiful. Each pupil bid hard-earned academic money of approximately $700 for a project contract that was worth $1,000 to $1,200, depending upon the excellence. If the buyer didn't fulfill his contract within the time limit allowed, he lost the contract and I auctioned it off again. So either way the buyer got a better education.

I also sold two teaching contracts, one in math and one in language. Each buyer was required to research thoroughly some approved subject in the academic area he purchased. Then a lesson plan had to be submitted to me for approval and suggestions, with time limits prescribed for every individual portion to be taught. And finally, the contract teacher was required to prepare an approved test covering everything he presented; give the examination to the whole class; and then either exchange papers in the classroom or correct the tests himself. My job, as the adult teacher, would be to act in an advisory capacity only.

Further, three rights to move the home seat to another location, two three-hour vacations, and one queen for a day were also sold, in that order. My bulletin boards were the final items offered for sale, just before the dismissal bell rang. I felt certain that school children had never before departed a classroom as charged up as mine were. Their excited conversation filled me with an eagerness to teach that is hard to describe. Every pupil brimmed with plans for future scholarly endeavors. At last, the academic money had a new worth and school work had an important meaning. I even heard Danny tell Henry that he would come over and they could help each other on some of the extra-credit projects available to any student who cared to take home a ditto sheet. How could anything be better? And I felt certain that, in time, an intrinsic love of learning would follow for some.

After everyone had gone, I sat at my desk and reflected on the system. Everything seemed to meet or exceed my expectations. And one thing was perfectly clear to me: this was the *only* way to teach. Some day, maybe I could communicate this information to many of my disillusioned colleagues. But probably the most exciting thing of all, which came as a result of the auction, was Bill's complete recapitulation. Before leaving he had begged my pardon and asked to be fully reinstated in the system. He and I both agreed that he should start with his bank account at zero.

Upon further reflection, I decided I was being prematurely enthusiastic. That night would tell the tale. It was "Back to School" night for parents and I would soon find out what they thought of the system. A shiver of fear ran down my spine. What if my parents flatly rejected the system? Could I ever again bring myself to teach conventionally? Was this the end of Harrison's teaching career? Now that I was really in love with my profession the thought of quitting made me ill. Well, no use making myself sick over what might never be. I shut the thought out of my mind, locked the door, and went home.

CHAPTER 8
A Teachers Meeting in the Lounge
Teacher Objections and Parental Support

Mr. T., the principal, had sent a note to all teachers prior to the afternoon dismissal bell advising them to be an hour early for the evening program. That would insure adequate instructor preparation and permit a very limited PTA meeting. I purposely arrived at the teacher's lounge fifteen minutes early with the hope that this would give me sufficient time to get a few intelligent and critical opinions on the system. At the time, it seemed wise to fortify myself with some friendly suggestions before facing a battery of possibly angry parents. But how wrong I was. I had reckoned without teachers' pride in their own ability and methods.

The lounge, as usual, was full of blue cigarette smoke. I knew that time was precious and I wasted none in preliminaries. The inner excitement of my new teaching discoveries had me deep into an explanation of the system before I knew it. Susan, my pretty listener, stopped me after a couple of minutes, her brown eyes shining with new-found interest. "Wait a minute, Al! This sounds terrific. How about sharing with the rest of the teachers? Wouldn't you like their opinions as well as mine?"

I nodded affirmatively and Susan stood to catch the necessary attention in the room. "Listen everyone! Al has developed some new teaching techniques which I think you will want to hear. He would appreciate your comments and suggestions. Okay, Al! Explain your system."

After Susan sat down I warned everyone that my explanation would take more time than we still had available. But at that moment, Mr. T. came into the room with the announcement that there would be no PTA meeting since the president was ill. He suggested that I continue with whatever explanation I planned to make. Thus encouraged, I began a sketchy description of the system's basics. In spite of the fact that only the bare bones of the system were revealed, it took me about fifteen minutes to give my listeners a working knowledge of the vast concepts involved. Interest ran high and I could see questions and frowns form as I covered the subject. My audience lost no time in putting voice to these at the end of my description. The first question came from a number of younger and less experienced instructors.

"Al! Don't you think your sysem is much too materialistic?"

One first-year teacher, more vocal than the rest, phrased it this way: "Are we ready to have the dollar take the number one spot in children's lives? What parent would want his child prepared for a total economic outlook on life?"

At first this attack caught me completely off guard, and I resented it until I remembered that I had specifically asked for just such opinions. I collected my thoughts and decided to use the very successful psychiatrist's technique of countering with a question.

"Just what is the purpose of our school system? I have always believed that our tax-supported school should prepare students for life as it is lived in the United States. The system I have proposed merely provides a convenient tool to duplicate our American society inside the classroom. Nowhere have I advocated a total financial outlook on life. Money in life or dollars in the classroom should be nothing more than a means to an end. Dollars can be instruments of sorrow or happiness. Even the Bible tells us that money isn't evil, it's the love of money that's bad. It is the duty of all educators to teach what is good and what is bad within any concept introduced in the classroom. I think it is a serious error to ignore such a golden opportunity and allow the pupil to learn economics only through the hard knocks of adulthood as we do now.

"Also, I feel that some of you may think that learning should be its own reward and that youngsters should learn to be motivated by a sense of duty instead of the extrinsic rewards offered in a system such as mine. If you think so, sit in any classroom, except where the talented are taught, and see how well this concept works. As an adult teacher, using the unique system that I have proposed, you could introduce the concept of duty in a natural atmosphere, where everything is not a duty the way it is in the conventional classroom."

I noticed, with relief, that some of my more respected colleagues were nodding in apparent agreement. One of the old timers brought out a question that I had expected, because it had occurred to me when I first conceived the system.

"What about the excessive competition involved with this type of program? Won't this prove harmful to pupils?"

"On the contrary!" I replied. "Students in my system may compete to whatever extent they desire and are never forced to produce beyond a well-defined minimum as they frequently are in the conventional classroom. My pupils produce academically at self-selected levels and are not stigmatized in any way because of a lack in ability. The slowest learner in my classroom may save his limited earnings and buy whatever company he desires. Students rapidly learn that anything is attainable through hard work rather than just the teacher's favor.

"The conventional classroom child must compete constantly for attention from his teacher and peers or else accept the role of a 'nothing,' day after day. With such recognition frequently based upon a nebulous reward from the sympathetic instructor, or else a socialistic 'your turn now!,' it is small wonder that students either give up and drop out or else have a nervous breakdown."

Now I really began to warm to my subject. "Pupils in my room, just as in real life, rapidly discover that the millionaire today may be broke tomorrow, especially after such an auction as we had today. Student teachers in one subject frequently become pupils in the next. There is constant interaction between students which will develop responsible citizens and leaders. In conventional classrooms, this type of responsibility, except for that owed to the teacher, is being strangled. If you doubt this just examine the characters and attitudes of your own pupils. How many exhibit the desirable traits that we boast as being the goals of a good education? Which of your students has become even minutely prepared to meet some of the practical aspects of modern day living? What child today understands the concepts of thrift or wasteful purchasing? Is there a child anywhere who has felt the degradation of bankruptcy or the thrill and sense of power and responsibility accompanying large amounts of money? How many know the true meaning of charity? And this names only a few.

"Competition *is* the American way of life. It made us great and the lack of it robs Russia of strength. I say that proper instruction in this vital subject belongs inside the classroom. Too many humans have crashed on the rocks of reality after floating on a classroom sea of make-believe utopia."

Suddenly aware of my excessive zeal, I apologized for the lengthy tirade and asked for further questions or objections. "Don't you feel that your system requires excessive extra work from the already over-burdened instructor?" This was offered by one of the other male teachers.

"No!" I replied. "The system, once learned, should give the teacher additional free time both at school and at home. The student teachers in the system provide assistance at the moment it is needed. This eliminates the customary dragging academic feet. Constant repetitive lessons should be a thing of the past.

"Instructors will find that increased motivation brings more rapid learning, and learning by experience doubles retention. I feel certain that adult teachers using this system will discover that their student teachers can improve the academic performance of the whole class. In fact, the adult teacher-pupil ratio might even be raised with no appreciable loss in educational values. Larger classes should mean a richer social environment for students, more opportunities for leader-ship training, and wider openings where self-reliance and creativity can be exercised with the most benefit. The small additional demands on the adult teacher's time should be limited to the few additional student teachers needed to operate with the larger number of children."

By now, I noticed some mouths hanging open. I decided to answer the question I could see forming. "No! I am not advocating that more pupils be dumped on the poor overworked teacher." I wisely realized that such a suggestion would not only immediately alienate my audi-ence but also brand me as a radical who was very dangerous to the profession. "Instead," I continued, "I am merely answering the ques-tion that was asked. The system will definitely not increase the teach-er's labors but rather provide additional moments for creative thought."

"It seems to me," remarked one of the older teachers labeled as the school dynamo, "that this method is a lazy way to teach. If the students do it all, why have a professional as the teacher? Wouldn't the janitor do as well?"

This brought forth the laughter and derision that it was designed to do. I cut into the merriment with my answer. "Any method that induces pupils to learn on their own should never be dismissed as a lazy way to teach. Self-motivation, I have always supposed, is the long-sought, but seldom-achieved, goal of every instructor. The teacher who doesn't possess the native inborn ability to motivate pupils can now resort to a successful method rather than trying hopelessly to change his personality to achieve this end."

"But I believe," the school dynamo interjected, her somewhat injured ego showing, "that your success as a teacher is not the result of any system or method you may use, but instead, is primarily due to your interpersonal relationship with your students."

"That," I replied, unable to completely restrain all of my derision, "is almost word for word from any student teacher's college manual."

"What if it is?" she countered, no longer caring to hide her dislike of either me or my system. "It's true, isn't it?"

"Only partially!" I answered with calm certainty, realizing that it would be a mistake to further antagonize her. "I agree that any teacher who has a barren relationship with his or her students can expect little in the way of success. This has been proven time and again with television instruction. However, excellent rapport with the kids does not necessarily assure success. To this, I think you will agree?"

Not waiting for an answer, I continued. "Not knowing any better remedy, many college instructors grasp at this concept as *the* solution to classroom troubles. It is convenient and plausable to blame poor rapport when difficulties occur. I say convenient because colleges are presently in the business of training teachers to interact with pupils on a personal basis. Teaching methods or systems are de-emphasized by stating that these are personal to each individual teacher. They say, 'what will work for one instructor will not for another.' Therefore, the teacher is left to devise his own.

"I believe that this is wrong. Isn't it much easier to develop a system suitable to most teachers rather than try to improve personalities? Once a program is successful for one teacher it should be studied for a wider application. Eventually a few systems could be taught to instructors which would insure some reasonable chance for success, with problems and results much more predictable and controllable. As it is now, those few teachers who are actually improved usually move out of the classroom into administrative positions or upward into the business world of large salaries."

Again I caught myself lecturing my audience. This wouldn't do, I knew, especially coming from a nobody who had hardly been in the classroom a week. I begged their pardon and asked for more questions.

Playfully, Mr. T. put up his hand. I smiled and nodded permission. "What about teacher and school liability with these student trips that you plan to sell at auction?"

"This should be no problem," I replied, "for any teacher or school district. The major danger lies in transportation. Approximately five children, once a month, can be driven to a preselected amusement area. The teacher should have adequate automobile passenger insurance. Personal liability protection while at the place of amusement should be three-fold. First, the business establishment normally carries insurance. Second, the teacher should purchase the inexpensive policy offered by most teachers associations. Third, the school district's insurance covers field trips that are frequently far more complex and costly than any sold in this system. Therefore, district officials should register no objections."

Mr. T. shook his head negatively. "I'm sorry to disagree with you where the school district is concerned. Maybe they shouldn't object, but based upon personal experience, I would bet my last dollar that they will."

And how right he was I would never know until many frustrating years later. But being new to mossbacked educational philosophies, I thought I could take reason in hand, right then and slay that nonsensical dragon. "I believe many of society's ills can be traced to improper use of our growing recreational time. People just don't know what to do with their ever-increasing spare moments. They turn to strong drink, sex, drugs and even crime in their search for new thrills and adventure. Why don't we educate people in the art of recreation? Not by showing them exactly how to put the heroin needle in, not by explaining which business gets robbed the most, or not by revealing where sex can be had for hire. Instead, let's give instruction in deep sea fishing, bowling, skiing, roller skating and all the other myriad amusements that people enjoy on their days off. It seems to me that people so educated would lead much more enjoyable lives. Happily many of our civic-minded organizations think so also, such as the Boy Scouts and others.

"Under the system I have just explained, teachers have the opportunity to teach this healthy concept and children have the opportunity to earn the right to participate in it, raher than have it come by way of a gift or from the 'my turn' concept. I firmly believe that something gotten for nothing is usually treated as worthless.

"Truly! It seems ridiculous to me that any school district would or could object to recreational education bought with donated teacher time. This is especially true when most school district taxpayers are constantly being asked to pay for vandalism at schools where the pupils don't know what else to do with their vacations.

"Some people may say that schools already have too much student recreational time and certainly don't need to teach more. But the actual fact is that little practical recreation *is* taught at school.

"Elementary school recesses are usually little more than supervised mayhem and most physical education periods are devoted to sports that have very little applicability when the child grows up. For I ask you, how many adults play soccer, baseball, football, volleyball, ring toss, or most of the other games taught?"

I could see the question forming in my listeners' faces, so I forestalled their asking it. "No! I *do not* think that physical education should be eliminated from the curriculum. Young bodies must be exercised and overworked minds should have a chance to unwind in competitive sports."

I looked around the room to be certain that I had not been misunderstood. Susan took advantage of my pause to ask a question. "What happens to the unfortunate teacher who chooses not to use your system? Isn't this unfair to her?"

To be certain that I thoroughly understood her question, I asked one of my own. "Unfair! In what way?"

"Well," Susan answered, "it seems unfair to force any teacher to compete with such a system as you have just described."

I surveyed my audience to observe their reaction. Many faces held the cornered and frightened look of those who feel their profession is threatened. I knew a sense of hopelessness but I still had to make an attempt to change their minds.

"I'm sorry if I hurt your feelings by saying this, but such thinking is the source of most of our present difficulties in education. Our wonderful free enterprise nation is being throttled inside the classroom by teachers thoroughly trained in socialistic methods." I heard some gasps of dismay before continuing.

"Everyone must be made equal. Nothing can ever be better than anything else. If it is, it must be degraded until it falls to the same shoddy level of its neighbors, and if it can't be so tarnished, it is eliminated altogether.

"Children are cautioned that it is only the group or society as a whole that rates improvement. Individualism is definitely taboo. The pupil who tries to be different frequently finds himself outside of the classroom door. Can we expect teachers themselves to be any different from the philosophies they pass on to their children?

"Certainly it's unfair to force any teacher to better himself by using a method he dislikes. Even more—it's criminal, since such a teacher under duress can and will make even the best of techniques seem inferior. But I ask you, in all fairness to society and its children, which will you do? Force the inefficient teacher to compete or force an inferior education upon defenseless children? As members of society and classroom instructors, the choice is clearly yours. But remember this, not you but rather future generations will pay the terrible price for your wrong decision now.

"I know that it is a very difficult thing that is asked. But in the last analysis, it *is* still fair. All teachers have the *opportunity to choose*, which is more than can be said for socialistic philosophies where everyone must conform to the will of the group."

After this tirade, my audience sat numb in their chairs. I felt a kind of creepy sensation at the back of my neck. Had I said too much? After all, I was a rank newcomer to the profession. What right did I have in lecturing veterans who were probably teaching at the time I was in elementary school? I was saved from the embarrassment of finding out by the clanging of the school bell.

With the spell broken, Mr. T. was the first to speak.

"Well!" he said, with a twinkle in his eye and the thousand dollar smile on his face, "Now that we have had our full ration of educational philosophy for the day, on which we can chew for the rest of the evening, I propose that you all depart for your respective classrooms and spoon feed some to the parents you will find waiting there."

Most teachers left laughing. At whom, I wasn't sure. The truly amazing thing, I thought, was how completely unconcerned everyone seemed, despite my best efforts. This, I decided, would probably be something I must learn to endure if I were to persist in the field of education. Surely my parents couldn't be any rougher on me than these teachers had been. And thank God, they weren't.

I spent a very pleasant fifteen minutes explaining the system to about twenty-five mothers and fathers. The remainder of the hour was devoted to simple questions and answers. Occasionally a parent would express enthusiasm over the increased academic motivation displayed at home as a result of the system. Many parents described phenomenal improvements which, at the time, I felt were just too good to be true, especially when the newness of the program was considered.

A few persons expressed concern about the same portions of the system that had distressed my colleagues. However there was this comfortable difference: the parents seemed to accept explanations with a much more open mind, and the general atmosphere remained calm and informative. But I also realized that this was to be expected since experienced educators could see problems that would not be visible to parents.

At 9:30 I locked the door and drove home with mixed feelings. I felt certain that most of my parents approved, but I also realized that some still had reservations. The reaction of my colleagues was another matter. I hoped my rapport with fellow teachers and my professional image had not been damaged beyond repair. Perhaps my colleagues viewed my lectures as the ravings of a madman who should be exorcised from the teaching profession. But more than likely their thoughts were not so drastic. I was probably considered just another harmless education crank who was just too young and inexperienced to turn their comfortable classroom world upside down as they thought I wanted to do. In either case, I knew that I had lost their esteem. This I must try to regain, but never at the expense of my own philosophies and ideals.

CHAPTER 9

The Next Month
Troubleshooting and Smoothing the System

For the next month of school I decided that it would be best to consolidate my gains and eliminate my errors rather than introduce further innovations. But this was difficult to do without inventing new methods. The system was so different that usual remedies would not work properly, just as the problems I encountered were frequently novel inside a classroom.

As an example, it didn't take long, with my enthusiasm, to overinflate the system. I gave excessive dollars for tests and homework whenever the terrific academic pace seemed to slacken. Not until I realized that such speed was really non-essential to a good education, did I tone down my monetary rewards. Then my pendulum of problems swung the other way. When little was accomplished because of the lack of a tangible recompense, I fined pupils for their failure. Finally I came to understand what was involved. Supply and demand were at work. I merely raised fines, auctioned more desirable items, and, in a general way, increased living costs. This usually brought our economy into line, and whenever it didn't, I developed enough patience to wait until it did, realizing that no matter what happened my pupils were still moving academically at twice the speed of the conventional classroom.

Perhaps the most difficult adjustment, for everyone, involved the need for increased emotional control. Court suits were many, with almost all settled out of court, until students learned to respect persons and their property. Even the old adult teacher was caught in such a legal tangle. I called one student a stupid jackass and shook him until his teeth rattled. I meekly settled out of court for three hundred dollars and made my victim so happy that he said he hoped I would forget and do it again. What the consequences would have been, if my classroom had operated conventionally, I shuddered to think. From that moment on, I tried to bridle my anger and collect damages from pupils. Thus, all of us would profit.

Another emotional state of mind I found difficult to develop was an inner callous attitude toward bankruptcy. As previously indicated, I outwardly sympathized with my students but sometimes my heart wept as well. I kept telling myself that the bankrupt pupil deserved what he got. He and he alone had put himself in a position where a better education could be forced upon him. But my tender nature always flinched as the poor unfortunate dropped deeper and deeper into debt where more schoolwork was demanded. So I planned some assistance.

Once I was truly convinced that the bankrupt pupil had learned his lesson, I used a partially satisfactory but somewhat shady method to bail him out. Occasionally I offered certain types of academic work, usually in the subject area where he was the weakest. His correct answers paid double or even triple the customary rates. When the other students complained and requested similar treatment, I would explain that this was only available to parolees in bankruptcy. I said that if anyone cared to enter bankruptcy and earn his parolee status, I would be glad to accommodate him. No one was interested in that.

From that idea flowed another welfare concept designed to spur certain academically retarded pupils. The actual procedure came to me one afternoon after spending almost an hour in a frustrating and unsuccessful attempt to teach Henry and Danny some of the more difficult multiplication tables. One minute they remembered and the next it was gone. I knew they were making the effort but little was accomplished. In desperation I played what I hoped to be my last trump card.

"I'll tell you what, boys," I said resignedly, "I'll give each of you ten dollars apiece for every new one you can learn by tomorrow, and if you also know them at the end of the week I'll pay a hundred dollars each."

It was almost worth the high cost just to watch their expressions and actions. First they were incredulous, then jubilant, and finally industrious. I didn't guess, I *knew*, that here was leverage worth further investigation. Why not apply the same economic pressure to some of our nonreaders like little Mary Brown? I called her to me.

"Mary, how would you like to earn triple the customary amount offered for every new vocabulary word you learn?"

Her shy smile told me all I needed to know. She worked at the word list I gave her like a beaver on a tree. Substantially the same offer was made to other academically weak pupils in most subjects. But as could be expected, my better pupils began to grumble about the unfairness. Why should their neighbors earn twice or three times as much for the same thing they did? And I had to acknowledge that they were right. It wasn't fair! Life itself didn't operate this way and it would be a disservice to teach otherwise. Nevertheless, at the time, I felt that the end justified the means and explained my actions in the following manner.

"How many students have ever seen a sailboat race?" Only one hand raised. "Well," I continued, "let me tell you that they have a method of handicapping the big ships or else the little ones would never have a chance. And this is what I have done in here. The handicaps will last for only a month. After this period everything will return to normal. So if you slow students ever intend to work on your weak areas this is the time to do it."

I noticed some of my top students still grumbling. Since I felt so guilty, I sought to pacify them with a bit of logic: "Some of you complaining hot shots have failed to recognize an important point. As student teachers, your one-fifth bonus will now be much larger since your slow pupils can earn more."

This seemed to turn the tide and the last resistance disappeared. But I have never felt comfortable nor right about using the handicap method. Continued use of such a technique would be like a rubber crutch in the sun when the going became rough and tough. No society anywhere can exist very long if a small minority is forced to support the majority. Just because I had an unlimited source of academic dollars was no excuse for giving them away unearned. Every pupil had to be taught to live with his handicap, or better yet overcome it, rather than use it as an excuse to freeload. With positive thinking even the slow learner can succeed.

Another problem developed from my generosity with our "Harrison dollars." The extra credit projects the kids achieved at home almost swamped me until I remembered an important part of my own advice when using the system—let the students do it!

An "Extra Credit Company" was sold to the highest bidder among the qualified buyers. Since life itself was our classroom pattern, only certain students, the top half of the class, were qualified to perform the highly technical work of correcting student papers. My students understood and accepted this concept just as everyone realizes the need for only qualified specialists in the professions. The Extra Credit Company leaseholder earned a tenth of whatever he processed and could hire an approved assistant whenever business became brisk. This effectively eliminated my work load and also enriched the checker's education.

In the same way I appreciated the service performed by the Bankruptcy and Probation Company. This classroom concern effectively supervised the education and activities of all impoverished students. It was the company's business to make certain that proper assignments were given to the indigent and that these were returned on time; that each penniless pupil was last in line and suffered any other indignity associated with his particular status; and finally, to inform the proper people of either the bankruptee's release or his entry into the very serious position of public enemy number one, two, or three.

A public enemy reached his infamous position by remaining in bankruptcy beyond a week. This status immediately necessitated a phone call to his parent with other drastic measures following, such as a parental visit with the adult teacher and even a short suspension from the classroom when no visible improvement was noted. Fortunately none of my pupils forced me to the more extreme punishments. Usually the discomfort of bankruptcy was sufficient.

All of the classroom companies provided all-day assistance to me in the many tedious and time-consuming tasks which plague most conventional teachers daily. For example, most students habitually fail to listen when instructions are offered and this gave rise, in my room, to the "Information Company."

Bill Bonehead was probably my worst offender in this respect. "All right, Bill!" I exclaimed one day when he had tried my patience beyond the breaking point. "You are going to pay for the privilege of sitting here fat, dumb and happy."

Actually Bill was just the opposite of my description and I could continue only after the class had its laugh. "I am going to auction off a lease for an 'Information Company.' It will be the business of this concern to sell repeated directions to any pupil who fails to listen when they are free." I followed through with a quickie auction. From that time onward I usually had the undivided attention of all pupils. But whenever I didn't, I couldn't have cared less and the nonlistener couldn't have cared more.

Most of the other effective companies came about in a similar fashion. The need gave rise to the innovation. For instance pupils would not usually have correct change whenever a fine was assessed. This brought forth a Change Company which made a small charge for the service it performed. The Book Company collected ten dollars daily for every reminder issued on overdue library books. It also earned profits from textbook rentals to the forgetful pupil who failed to bring his own from home. The Inspection Company came into being after excessive errors were discovered in the exchange examination papers. When slipshod correction errors came to five dollars each, my pupils made few. And from the need for new classroom companies itself arose a business. The Patent Company was licensed to issue "invention certificates" for any classroom creativity which was commercially marketable.

One area of trouble that I experienced could never occur in the conventional classroom. The ingredients to create the problem were nonexistent except in the Harrison System. I discovered this malady quite by accident. Danny was usually in and out of bankruptcy, since his talking was very expensive and his work habits were profligate. He frequently handed in two hundred dollars worth of homework and then spent it by the end of the school day. That was his usual pattern, but for some strange reason he began to drop deeper and deeper into bankruptcy. I decided it was time to investigate and took him aside for questioning.

"What's happening to all of your money, Danny?"

Danny's eyes turned down and he scraped around in the dirt with his shoe edge. "Gosh, Mr. Harrison! I just can't tell ya. If Henry even knew I was talking to you now, he would be mad."

"Henry?" I said, surprised. "What has he to do with it?"

"Oh!" Danny replied, his surprise as evident as mine. "I thought somebody had already told you about what he did."

"Well!" I said, making my voice stern enough to achieve the desired results. "You have said enough for me to insist on an explanation."

"Please, Mr. Harrison!" Danny's face had the stricken features of the cornered. "I just can't tell ya. Henry will beat me to a bloody pulp."

"Danny," I replied, softening my tone just a little, "Do you know what a 'court injunction' is?" When he shook his head negatively, I continued. "It's an order from the judge to do, or not to do, something. When it's issued it has the effect of a law and anyone disobeying it can be fined. Well, I'm going to issue two injunctions. One for you to explain and the other for Henry to keep his hands off you. Whichever of you violate this court order, that person will pay a $500 fine. So now please go on with your explanation, for Henry will bother you no more."

Despite my definite assurances, Danny looked around the playground evidently to be certain that Henry wasn't near.

"Well, O.K.!" he said in a low voice. "But if he lays a finger on me I can also sue him, can't I?"

His expression pleaded for an affirmative answer, and he waited for my confirming nod before proceeding. "I suppose you remember how mad Henry got with me a few weeks ago?" Again he waited for my affirmation which I gave. "Well, Henry agreed not to pound me up after school if I paid him a hundred dollars each night. So I have been collecting cash for my extra credit and giving it to him in the evening."

As Danny progressed with his tale my mouth gradually hung open further and further. Here was the old extortion racket, full blown, right in my classroom. But why should I expect my classroom problems to be different than those in life? Wasn't my system supposed to be a slice of life tailored to youngsters? What would be more natural than this? The savage tribes did the same thing to their neighbors and modern men have always extorted money in just a little more sophisticated manner. Therefore, it seemed best that the solution should be patterned after society's, and I would welcome the opportunity to teach it.

First, I immediately issued a directive to the banker which prevented cash payments to any present or future bankruptee until an official release was given. Second, I put Henry under a $1,000 "peace bond," which I fully explained to the class before it was invoked. Third, a classroom law was passed covering similar situations and Henry was made to realize how fortunate it was for him that it couldn't be made retroactive. Fourth, Danny was advised of his rights at law regarding the possibility of a civil suit against Henry for the recovery of his extortion money.

Henry quickly settled out of court and Danny, fortunately for

Henry, agreed to accept an IOU. Thus, saved from certain bankruptcy, even Henry seemed pleased with the developments. I felt that the lesson learned by everyone was worth a dozen academic assignments. The time loss was insignificant if it prevented even one such serious crime in the future. Pupils had to learn to become fully responsible for all of their acts. I felt pleased that my unique teaching methods allowed most criminal deviations to appear at a stage in life where their corrections can be made with a minimum of harm.

Probably my greatest difficulty in using the system was routine for any adult who instructs children, be he parent, teacher or preacher. I wasn't as consistent as I should have been. Luckily for me the system has a natural built-in requirement for fairness and justice which forced me to become consistent. I couldn't very well fine one pupil for breaking the law and not another. My students would immediately speak up and demand that I take the lawbreaker's money.

With so much happening within the system, and sometimes all at once, it was difficult for me in the beginning to be as consistent as possible. Gradually I improved as I learned to employ more student assistance. At first, my natural adult pride kept me from accepting advice and suggestions from mere children. This attitude was radically changed for me one day when I was absent and forgot to turn off the system for my surprised adult substitute. The children operated the classroom so expertly that the sub raved about it in the teacher's lounge. Naturally, I heard all the nice things the next day and decided to call on the individual at his home that night.

His comments were complimentary, to say the least. Never before had he seen such self-reliance and self-discipline inside a classroom. I left with a warm glow in my heart and a determination to experiment even further with some of the more difficult and deeply disturbing maladies now bothering the nation, such as racial and ecology problems, and others even more complex. Some would perhaps require the remaining seven months to develop new attitudes among my pupils. But I was now convinced that I had the tools and only needed the time.

CHAPTER 10

For the Rest of the Year
Teaching Large Remedial Concepts

A couple of months passed before I actually visualized the full scope and potential of the system. Gradually I began to satisfy myself that our American society and many of its concepts could be reproduced inside my classroom. And what was perhaps even more important, I now believed that each situation could be tailored to the minds of my children.

The group work with student teachers offered many hidden learning opportunities beyond leadership training and instant aid to the slow. The interaction of pupils in their group work permitted everyone to experience the type of intimate association normally offered only to adults in their workaday world. I observed student reactions as they gradually turned from derision to respect.

Who would have ever thought Henry capable of teaching anyone anything? Yet, Henry earned and kept a number five science teachership and finally became more respected for his practical assistance to pupils than the number one instructor. Even some of my more racially conscious caucasian children pleaded with Henry to be admitted to his interesting science group.

Here, it seemed to me, was a good solution to the racial problem, before unreasonable attitudes could become fossilized. When black Henry could exhibit academic prowess in the classroom, as well as physical strength on the ball field, not many children were going to pay much attention to the color of his skin. And any student who thought otherwise was due for a surprise. I actually overheard Henry make this statement to a fellow bankruptee as they both sat in the back of the classroom doing scheduled homework: "Gosh, my bank account is sure sick! I just wish someone would call me a 'nigger' so I could sue 'em."

The most obvious advantage of the system was its ability to teach economic concepts. However, to what extent this could be done, even I never fully realized until a number of months had passed and certain dilemmas had arisen. Jim, our banker, gradually became the room's tycoon. He bought business after business and had quite a large staff working for him. Some of the pupils became jealous of his wealthy position and decided to cut him down to size. Two students made the claim that he was stealing from the bank and they caused an audit to be run on all transactions during the month. This was permissible and carried out at recess time. Jim came through the audit with an unblemished record and then he retaliated with a court suit against the accusing girls, which he won. Thus, Jim increased his wealth at his antagonists' expense and prevented further unfounded claims and grumbling.

At first I felt that there was nothing wrong with Jim's strongly acquisitive instinct. When it continued, until he was considered a first-class miser, I became alarmed. Finally, I determined to step in and teach him a lesson, but an adequate opportunity never arrived until the end of the school year.

Jim possessed well over sixty thousand dollars by this time, which was twice the bank account of his nearest competitor. For the previous two months, he had worked like a dog on academic work and had squeezed the last dollar from his business enterprises. He had begun to deny himself drinks, except at recess, and had even been caught begging stubs of pencils from friends rather than pay the $150 for a new one. He had succumbed to the "money game."

The most available and most valuable auctionable item that I could find for the last day of school was, quite naturally, money. It fits every student's needs. I brought two dollars in nickels and dimes. The auction started with a dime.

"I've got a thousand dollars," I began. "Two, five, ten and now twenty thousand dollars. Going once, twice, three times, and sold to Big Jim." I had my chance at last and I used it profitably. "Say, Jim! How many arithmetic problems or spelling words would you have to do for ten thousand dollars? Very many?" I waited for Jim to nod his head vigorously. "Well, tell me, would you have done that much work for a dime?"

Suddenly Jim stopped examining his newly acquired coin and reacted to my question. His eyes went wide and his mouth dropped open. "My Gosh! I just did, didn't I?"

The whole class laughed with him.

The lesson was far more poignant than any lecture I could have devised. But I still couldn't resist the temptation to deliver a small sermon on the evils of becoming a miser and treating money as a god rather than what it actually is, a mere tool of man.

Another social problem took about six months to appear. The first classroom monopoly was also engineered by Tycoon Jim. He owned Information Company number one when I sold number two for the free enterprise purpose of forcing his excessive charges downward. Not over two days passed before Jim had negotiated a financial agreement with the owner of number two. Again, the price of information went up in both establishments. Frustrated, I decided to auction off one more. It took me a week to discover that Jim had bought number three through well paid agents. Prices were soaring once more.

I was faced with two alternatives, either government price regulation or government operation. In my mind, one evil was as bad as the other. Finally, I settled for auctioning off company number four, on a day when Jim was absent. This concern was licensed with the restrictive provision that no charge of this new company could be more than half that estimated by any other information company. This meant that any pupil wishing to do business with number four must first get a quote from one of the other three. Naturally, this effectively put Jim and his cohorts out of business. A fine lesson was learned by everyone in the room. But this still didn't really satisfy me. I waited until Jim returned the next day before discussing the evils of monopoly. We finished the informative session by passing a restrictive law against any future monopoly bent on price controls or fleecing the public.

If I had been asked to point out the single most valuable aspect of the economic concepts taught by the system, my choice would have been the program's ability to foster free enterprise principles. Once upon a time, a hundred years ago and before, people understood and valued what free enterprise meant. Today, the term has almost become lost in the socialistic atmosphere of the classroom and in the security-minded society which follows. To illustrate, I had one of my parents take me to task after the "back to school night."

"Mr. Harrison! I just don't understand why you would want to teach free enterprise principles. With all these welfare and giveaway government programs available, kids certainly don't need to learn how to get anything *else free.*"

And how right she was! As I explained the term free enterprise for her benefit, I began to realize, myself, just how weak we all are in understanding and using our system.

For instance, how often can anyone be induced to risk even his time, let alone money, on anything but a guaranteed sure thing? How many lenders will risk money without the customary government guarantee? What house can be built unless the building department assures its proper construction? Even the land itself must be zoned to guarantee the right kind of neighbors. And what about farm subsidies, cost-plus, etc.? The list of initiative-robbing guarantees grows larger every year until even the air we breathe is about to be guaranteed.

Noticing that in my excitement I was becoming more and more militant, I apologized to my listener, and admitted to another side of the coin.

"The crux of today's troubles, I feel, lies in the inability of conventional classrooms to teach individual responsibility rather than the collectivism drilled into every pupil. A student, responsible to himself and God, can be taught to look out for his neighbor." Eventually I persuaded the parent that modern man had lost most of his ability to assume risks, and some form of instruction seemed to be needed.

A few of my pupils bought businesses that lost money. Some of these losers expected refunds and even asked their parents to intercede in their behalf. Patiently I explained that business reverses are the everyday lumps which adult businessmen face. And any unbeliever had only to ask a local businessman for confirmation. In fact, I promised a refund to any pupil who could induce a local merchant to say that he thought the student was deserving after hearing all of the circumstances. I never had to return a dollar.

With the hope that I could induce pupils to broaden their education and learn to enjoy venturing forth, I organized the Stock and Bond Company. Students researched the processes and products of many real companies prior to investing their hard-earned academic dollars. Not only did this enrich knowledge but it also taught pupils something about the stock market. Parents would tell me, with amazement, how they frequently had to fight with their son or daughter for the financial page in the local newspaper.

Hand in hand with the concept of venturing had to go a program to encourage thrift. The old adage of "a fool and his money are soon parted" had as much application in my classroom as when it was first spoken. For what purpose would pupils risk their all only to lose it the next minute? We developed a Finance Company to lend money at 20 percent per month interest. Borrowing privileges at a 10 percent rate were also extended to this concern by a *true* Federal Reserve System, namely me. Thus the large percentages encouraged everyone to use his own money. At first the naive child viewed this company as an inexhaustible storehouse of free funds. Fortunately, perhaps, for the student who hadn't good collateral (either a good work record or a leased company), the financier turned a deaf ear to his pleas. But eventually even the poor risks became enmeshed in the coils of debt. It was really painful to watch.

Danny was the first to be snared and he poured forth his woe at recess time. "Mr. Harrison! How come I seem to work my toenails off and never pay back much more than just the interest on the money I've borrowed?"

I selected this as our topic for discussion when everyone returned to the room. After the realities of borrowing had been spotlighted, most students hated to believe that anyone, including themselves, could be so stupid. Thereafter, patterns were reversed and many took advantage of the savings program offered at 5 percent interest. Some still continued to borrow, but on a much more selective basis. Most loans were now negotiated to invest in a business that would make more money, while personal savings usually bought pleasure items.

Writing about debt now leads me to one of the most serious problems confronting the modern world—welfare. How I handled this malady in my classroom should please most overtaxed citizens. A classroom non-profit foundation was formed to dispense charity. Whenever pupils who lacked funds had a pencil stolen, required excessive restroom trips for medical reasons, or required money for other charitably sound ventures, the foundation stood ready to finance them. Foundation income depended upon contributions from students, usually those who died.

Oh yes! My pupils died if they were transferred from my room. And like life itself, "you can't take it with you," so this called for a will.

The will could not be executed until the day of transfer, and any pupil who divulged his intent prior to the reading of the instrument, negated the will. This helped prevent children from buying friends and kept the departing pupil hard at work until the last moment. Some students made their departing parents wait as much as thirty minutes while they finished a particular math or spelling page. In the children's minds, the larger the legacy, the higher they expected to stand in the others' estimation, and the longer they would be remembered. Despite their own awareness of their forgetfulness, I could never convince them of the truth in the old adage, "out of sight—out of mind." They continued to accumulate an education, and as their teacher, I couldn't be anything but happy. However, one part of their thinking did change as they observed the big bite "inheritance taxes" took from each individual gift. Very soon, most pupils decided that a donation to the foundation was just as effective and far less debilitating. Gifts to the foundation were tax-free.

As the Bible tells us, we are basically self-centered. The contributions naturally dwindled to a mere pittance. Few students transferred, and selfishness grew with the auctions. Finally the day came when little Susie Brown had her textbook stolen and, coming from a very poor family, had no actual spare cash in her home to purchase another. Clearly, here was a job for the foundation. I agreed to provide the necessary fifty cents cash if I could be paid ten academic dollars for every penny I donated. The class agreed that this would be fair and the foundation directors voted to appropriate the necessary $500. But a quick check revealed an empty foundation treasury.

"Well, class!" I said sadly. "What do you recommend that we do?"

Danny's hand shot up from the back of the room. I nodded, expecting the worst.

"It's like you said, Mr. Harrison. We should look to real life for solutions in here. There's only one thing you can do. You're going to have to tax all of the stingy-guts in the room who won't give when they got it."

This brought forth a mixture of levity and serious dissent. The more knowledgeable students could visualize what this would do to precious bank accounts. Despite the disturbance Danny had caused, I wanted to go over and hug him. I felt that I couldn't have said it better myself. But instead of embracing Danny, I settled for a compliment.

"Danny, sometimes you are so sharp it's almost unbelievable."

Danny's grin went from ear to ear and his chest puffed up in pride. Right after that I put on my most lamentable face and proceeded to assess each student's bank account for Susie's welfare bill. When the tax money was collected, we discussed the newly discovered reasons why charity should be put high on our list of desirable human attributes. There were no unbelievers that day, only a few more bank-ruptees.

But probably the zenith of the tax picture was reached in the spring. When the "graduated income tax" chewed up the major portion of the production from my most industrious pupils, the cry of pain almost rattled the windows.

"Why should I work hard," John wailed, "when you take over half of what I make?"

"Half, nothing!" Jim moaned. "You should see what that stinking income tax has done to the profits from my businesses."

"I'm not ever going to work again!" I heard Danny tell Henry. "What's the use? If I'm going to work for the government, they're going to pay me, not me pay them for the privilege."

But actually, this was only half of my planned lesson. I had specifically waited until we had plenty of bankruptees. "Now," I said, "as governor of this classroom I shall use this tax money for the welfare of our bankruptees." My voiced oozed compassion. "The poor unfortunates of this room have suffered enough. Each will be bailed out of bank-ruptcy this one time and given a fresh start in life."

I couldn't determine which bellowed the loudest, my about-to-be-released debtors or the industrious pupils paying the bill. After turning the card to red, I gave Henry permission to speak.

"Mr. Harrison! This isn't right! Those bankruptees deserve to be where they are. If they weren't so lazy, and didn't cause so much trouble in here, they could get out on their own. I know, because I used to be the same until I got the message."

Beautiful! I thought. But instead, I acted just the reverse. "Why Henry! Would you have wanted that kind of thing said about you when you were down and out?"

"No, I probably wouldn't, then." Henry's eyes rolled upward and he became thoughtful. "But I'm sure glad now that I worked my own way out. It taught me a lot."

"I'm sure it did," I replied smiling in spite of myself. "All right! Suppose we ask the class for a better suggestion?"

"Not collect it in the first place!" Danny exclaimed loudly. I held out my hand and he promptly paid the required fine.

"That is undoubtedly the best advice," I said to the whole class. "But now that the government already has the money, how shall it be spent in relation to bankruptees?"

Jim raised his hand and I called on him. "I would suggest that if the funds can't be returned, they should be used for work projects that would benefit everyone in the room. For instance, the bankruptees could be paid for cleaning the blackboard, picking up paper at the end of the day, and even for writing special projects which would give us a better education."

I complimented Jim for his excellent ideas. Thus came into being our WPA (Willing Pupil Assistance) fund. Extra dollars were now available to any bankruptee who demonstrated a burning desire to elevate himself from the hated status.

The next large concept I learned to teach, by using the unique characteristics of the system, came as a natural outgrowth of the WPA. Whenever the classroom needed cleaning at the end of the day, the WPA funds paid bankruptees for their efforts. Quite naturally, there was a loud protest registered by the Clean-up Company whose business it was to warn pupils about dirty areas and then collect a fine from any who refused to listen. But this feeble objection was brushed aside by the large majority who felt that a few must suffer to benefit so many.

Thereafter, with such public largess, pupils grew extremely lax in their cleanliness. Nobody really cared when they had "free" clean-up. What were bankruptees for but to pick up trash? Rapidly the appropriated WPA funds disappeared and I was forced to approach the subject of income taxes once more.

"But why do we need the WPA?" Jim asked heatedly. "If everybody cleans his own area, no taxes are necessary. I don't throw *my* paper on the floor, now!" Jim stared meaningfully at his neighbor, Paul. "Why should I have to pay everybody else's bill?"

Paul raised his hand and I nodded. "Why shouldn't he pay? He's got plenty of money." Paul glared back at Jim.

Jim's reply was classic. "That's the trouble with too many people today. Those that have nothing expect everything from those who have something. Paul doesn't want to lose his soft government job as WPA coordinator so he expects working people like me to support him."

I had been waiting for this and I encouraged my class into a discussion. We talked about the scattered trash in our normally beautiful parks, and most pupils came to understand that it was everybody who paid for the mess of a few. We looked at the pollution of rivers by big business and decided that all businesses should finance water purification. It was revealed that any waste of public resources destroyed each person's tiny portion. Finally the class realized that individual responsibility was the best in the long run and the government-sponsored WPA died a natural death. The Clean-up Company once again resumed its duties.

But my most opportune moment to teach the lesson of waste and ecology arrived about a week later. Mr. Turner informed me that some members of my class had made a terrible mess in the boys restroom which the custodian would have a hard time cleaning. Mr. T. didn't know who the boys were, specifically, but reliable information placed the blame on my students. I approached the subject with the whole class but I could get no admissions. Everyone agreed that it was our responsibility to clean it. But who would do the job? The logical choice was the Clean-up Company. However, who would pay the bill? Finally it dawned on everyone. Taxes again! After this, all waste became everybody's business. I watch with delight as students took each other to task for abuses of public property which, previously, would have gone unnoticed. Here was individual responsibility at its best.

I hesitate to write about the next large concept capable of being adequately taught with my techniques. The subject of government is a sore and touchy area. It generates more arguments even than religion. Most conventional teachers succeed in ignoring it, especially in the child's early education where it can most easily be learned. When opinions have hardened in high school and college, instructors usually face dogmatic blank walls. Such curriculum planning, I feel, has dire consequences for our nation.

On a Friday afternoon toward the end of the school year, I copied all bank accounts on a separate piece of paper. Then I hid the sheet in one of my desk drawers, locked the door, and went home.

"A revolution has taken place," I announced to my class Monday morning. The "teacher's pet" was directed to draw six student names from a hat. These randomly picked pupils were to become our newly-appointed "Communist Party members" who would control everything inside the classroom.

With my guidance, the party immediately froze all bank accounts. The bank totals for each were juggled until everyone had the same amount and the surplus was siphoned into the government treasury. In effect, the party took from the rich and gave to the poor by making everybody equal except for the government which, naturally, took the lion's share.

As could be expected, cries of pain came from the formerly wealthy but were drowned in the majority's ocean of joy. Most comments contained the feeling that Communism might not be so bad after all. Paul made a statement fairly typical of the rest. "It's about time Tycoon Jim was cut down to size. He couldn't possibly spend all that money anyway."

However, on the whole, most pupils did appreciate the unfairness but not to the extent of refusing this sudden windfall. Much more surprising was the small protest registered by those hurt the worst. With the exception of a few of the very wealthiest, most losers felt constrained to silence rather than appear selfish to the majority. I overheard one pupil say: "Let the leaches have it; I can make some more!"

The next recess, again with my contrivance, all companies were socialized. When students returned to the room they were told of the new developments.

From then on each company would be owned by the state and every businessman would receive a salary, usually about a fourth of his former profit.

"But I paid a thousand three hundred dollars for the Pencil Company!" John yelled, disregarding our normal classroom rules in his anger. "Who's going to pay me for that?"

"That's nothing to what I've got invested!" bellowed Tycoon Jim.

When informed that there would be no compensation given, even Danny put in his two cents, despite the well-known fact that he hadn't owned a company for some time. "This seems more like stealing, legally, if ya ask me."

"Well they're not going to steal my company!" Henry said loud enough for all to hear. "I'll knock 'seven bells of Hell' out of anybody that tries."

I hushed them all with a wave of my hand, overlooking the universal infractions of the law, and I turned the card on red before speaking.

"I want you all to realize that this is much the way things might happen if we had a Communist takeover here. First of all, Henry, you aren't going to 'knock seven bells' out of anything, any more than you would if this were the real thing. As the enforcer of this room, I can be compared to the armed forces found in the Communist countries, such as the army, navy, airforce, police and secret police. Anyone disobeying the law makes himself subject to being sent to the 'Salt Mine.' This means that you can be sentenced to copy so many pages in the dictionary on your free time. And as the adult teacher in this room, believe me, I will see that you do every page of it." I made my visage as stern as possible and turned it on Henry, who, remembering my last tantrum, slipped a little deeper into his seat.

But in spite of my warning, I learned two weeks later that Henry's threat had caused two party members to be brought to school by their parents. Henry told the two girls that he would "pound them to a pulp," and in Henry's mood, they weren't about to doubt it. After the next recess we held our election for the executive, legislative and judicial branches of our Communist government.

"Mr. Harrison! How come only the party members can run for any office?" Danny asked about half way through the elections. "What good is it to vote if I can't ever be elected?"

"Good questions," I replied. "The only answers I can give are the same as those offered in the Communist countries. You just aren't qualified to run the government. Only the party members are."

"Well how can I get qualified?" Danny persisted.

"Get picked by the party members." I offered.

"But why should they pick me?" Danny replied, sagely. "They got that whole government treasury to spend, just between the six of 'em."

"Ah, ha!" I exclaimed. "Now you've got the picture. Everybody in Russia votes. In fact it's a crime if they don't. But only about one-sixth of the nation can hold office. These are the party members, who become such by invitation of the established members. Therefore, five-sixths of a Communist nation become what is in effect slaves to those who control everything."

Henry sought permission to speak and I granted it. "But why don't they revolt? Nobody would treat me like that, at least not forever."

"Good thinking, Henry," I answered. "But what would you do about it, anymore than you have in this classroom? You don't want to go to the 'salt mine,' or be shot in a Communist nation, so you do what you're told. However, it usually never comes to this, except for a tiny minority of troublemakers. The majority of people in a Communist country feel that they are better off than they were before, which is the way most of you felt in here at first. In a manner of speaking, the slaves are well treated, almost as well as party members, for it is in the best interest of the party to keep the majority happy and working for Communist causes. But there is this huge difference. Freedom, opportunity and initiative are gone, completely for the slaves and partially for the party members. These things that we hold so dear have been replaced by fear, force and apathy throughout the Communist part of the world."

About two days of communism was all my class could stand. After the first day I announced that the present party members would be replaced by six new ones so that more pupils could experience both sides of the picture. With the changeover, Danny became a party member and he expressed his delight very vocally.

"Man-o-man! This is great. No wonder the commies in Russia like it."

"That's right, Danny," I replied, "as a party member only. But never forget what it was like when the shoe was on the other foot. And believe me, everything can change overnight, just as it did in here."

And before the day was out, Danny made my prophesy come true. His sense of power went to his head. He exercised it so ruthlessly that he almost forced Henry into a fistfight. Finally a majority party vote expelled him.

At the end of the second day of communism I told the class that the next day we would move out of this form of government into a full dictatorship. A loud cheer of relief escaped from most throats. They had had enough. Many felt that anything would be better than the injustices suffered at the hands of those they had formerly called friends.

The following day I selected Henry for our classroom dictator. He was the perfect choice. Being the strongest and most fearless in the room, he could enforce, with my approval, any decision that he cared to make. Also he was emotionally ripe and ready for the position. Both Communist parties had misused him every way possible, at least in Henry's mind, and he was itching to get even.

I needed to warn pupils with an explanation of my moves as I made them. Forearmed is forewarned. "Usually the way a dictator comes into power is through the approval, connivance, and active support of the particular country's enforcement agencies. Unless the police and armed forces are behind him, the dictator's revolution usually fails. As in here, I am supporting Henry, so he is now your dictator."

Bill's hand raised and I nodded.

"Why did you select Henry?"

"Because I feel that he will do the kind of job I have in mind," I replied, smiling.

"Actually," I continued, "a dictatorship is easier to install when the majority of the people are dissatisfied, as they now are in this classroom. Most of you are ready to demand and accept almost any change that will control the undesirable elements. You will probably ask him to control the Communists and change the system, and he will be eager to do so. But like everybody else, you forget that the one who controls is not about to leave *you* uncontrolled just because you asked."

Henry took over the classroom in a typically despotic manner. He ran everything. When protests were lodged, the complainer was hustled off to the Salt Mine. Soon Henry had most pupils fit to be tied. He thoroughly enjoyed himself at the expense of the class. Only his favorites were picked for government office and all who displeased him had their bank account confiscated. A few of his worst enemies he forced into "concentration camp," nothing more than an isolated desk in a corner of the room where certain distasteful academic work was completed.

Before long I had many pupils begging for Henry's execution. So I schemed with them for his overthrow, and the plot was launched after the noon lunch recess. At 1 p.m. Henry found himself in the same concentration camp that he had so blithely decreed for others. The lesson that all learned was complete. The class was now ready for a democratic republic, a type of government for which I had hopefully been grooming them since the start of the school year. But first, I used my secret copy of the previous Friday's bank accounts to restore lost funds.

We elected all branches of government with a five-party system, all equally financed by taxes. Each party presented its campaign platforms. There were two senators, North and South, and a representative from each row of seats in the room, who were responsive to the wishes of their respective constituents. Lawmakers in our room usually caucused their voters before deciding any issue, since government employees considered the wishes of the majority or else ran the risk of impeachment or recall.

After this week of political experience, no one needed to tell my students which type of government was the best. Instead, most pupils told any stranger who would listen. The next school year, one of my colleagues confirmed the retentive value of the lessons by reporting to me how two of my former pupils had taken strong issue against communism when it was presented in his classroom. The dear fellow gave me a good feeling for the rest of that day.

Undoubtedly, the largest drawback to the system is also its greatest boon—the size. Almost any real life concept can be taught inside the classroom, but teaching the system to the instructor may seem like an impossible task. Actually, this is normally not true since the techniques of operation are no more complicated than the establishment of a merit monetary program for purchasing rewards for the children. Yet, in any explanation of the system, hours can be spent describing unusual methods which are customarily unavailable to the conventional teacher.

As an example, in the beginning the classroom bulletin boards wasted much of my time. They required constant attention to be kept current and neat. Finally, I got smart and leased them to the highest bidder for a month. The buyers did a great job and enriched their education at the same time. Also, I had to honestly admit that more of my pupils looked longer at these student-decorated boards than any I had put up.

Another unique advantage was offered to my slow children while outside of the classroom. The top half of my class, in each major subject, earned the right to tutor the lower half at home. This could be accomplished any evening the two pupils chose, and in some cases, it could be continued inside the classroom. Parents would write to me in their amazement. "John worked with Dave on arithmetic for two hours last night. If I hadn't seen this myself, I wouldn't have believed it. This system of yours is great." A parental note such as this earned that home tutor two dollars a minute, or $120 for the evening.

Not only did this technique advance education but it also developed harmonious working relations. Even Henry and Danny helped each other quite often, and when I received a note that Jim had helped Paul, I really knew it was successful.

The system, for me, was somewhat of a paradox. It allowed me to reach and motivate almost everyone during the year, but it also gave me more free time, rather than less. Big elaborate teaching preparations were unnecessary. In some cases I found that extensive window dressing merely clouded the lesson. Basically, being a lazy teacher, I hated all of the extensive research required for proper learning. The system allowed me to hand this distasteful chore to my students. They paid for the privilege and received a splendid education besides. This left me free to supervise and guide many pupils until even this task was bought by some ambitious student. He became the projects consultant for our room, and earned a fee for his valuable services.

Another desirable aspect of the system, I found, is its ability to be utilized piecemeal. The instructor can use whatever he wishes and leave the rest. This provides the flexibility required for universal application. As an example, I hate to do homework, while some instructors enjoy correcting reams of test papers outside of the classroom. This being the case, I decided to develop a technique for correcting all daily spelling and writing errors during the classroom day. Corrected examinations and work papers were not thrown away, but instead were filed in each individual's personal folder. At the end of every nine weeks, or report card period, all material was first reviewed by the owner, and then the owner's respective spelling teacher, for misspelled words. The owner could correct errors by respelling each word above the mistake. Any uncorrected error, after this, was fair game for the spelling teacher, who then collected a dollar a word from the pupil as well as ten correct spellings for every mistake. Both the student teacher and the pupil learned. Sloppy daily writing was handled in a similar fashion. Soon everybody realized that the message was there to read and heed—"try harder to write it correctly the first time!"

Early in the school year, I was somewhat concerned about the possible effect the system's competition might have on pupils, despite the indifference I described to my colleagues in the teacher's lounge. It appeared not only possible, but probable, that some students might develop more than a money game syndrome. This seemed especially true after inaugurating our competitive academic companies.

Students brought in many reams of paper on which they had written thousands of spelling words, vocabulary words, or arithmetic problems. The individual companies processed these and gave so many dollars for each production. All three businesses also gave speed tests on the knowledge gained in the writing. The fortunes made were exceeded only by the students' rapid progress. Yet, to all of the participating pupils, the whole process was nothing but fun.

Parents told me of children who now refused to go out to play. Instead, their child preferred to write spelling words or do division. It was unbelievable how much he or she had changed, they said.

One day I asked the formerly lazy Danny, "Why?"

"Well, Mr. Harrison! It's like this. Nobody forces me to do anything, anymore. If I don't want to work, I don't have to. But whenever I think about the money I'm losing while I'm playing, I just can't have as much fun. So I hate to quit working and play. Once I get started, I sometimes write spelling words until my mother makes me go to bed. There's no way to earn money any easier."

Nevertheless, it required about half of the school year before I really began to relax. Evidently my theories were well founded after all. The system did allow children to seek their own levels of production and didn't generate pressures beyond those I desired. However, my observation of a few supercharged students did induce me to begin a program designed to promote emotional maturity. I knew that additional knowledge in this sadly neglected subject was sorely needed. When doctors all over the country admitted that 50 percent of the illness they treat is emotional, it seemed more than appropriate to teach something about emotional maturity in the classroom.

I have long felt that the crux of many educational problems lies in a lack of tools, such as real-life experience. But what conventional teacher can or wants to duplicate the life situation causing a mental disturbance? Most instructors are careful to shelter their charges from such a trying experience. They even decry grades for this same reason. Every method possible is utilized to sweep the terrifying social malady under the educational rug. Many educators believe that tender egos must not be exposed to the harsh realities of life, yet, they helplessly watch their end products crash on the rocks of reality.

I made up my mind that this unhealthy situation should be remedied in my classroom. But the big question was how? I could not become personal in my methods the way they do in sensitivity and encounter groups. That properly belonged outside of the elementary school sphere. Clearly, the instruction had to be of the self-help and do-it-yourself variety. The first step required that I read some good books on the subject, which I did. Next I needed to apply the incentives in my system to achieve the desired goals. At the time, this appeared more difficult than it was, but finally I found the magic formula.

First, we discussed a different large emotional concept every week to determine its strengths and weaknesses. As an example, competition was dissected for its good and bad points, and then the next week the art of giving rather than receiving was examined for its numerous values.

Second, fines were established for any pupil who displayed an undesirable characteristic we had discussed, and rewards were offered for the reverse. For instance, Henry paid out much money in fines (as well as by court direction) for his uncontrolled anger, until he learned to bridle his emotions and return kindness for injury. The results amazed even him as he related a few examples for the class.

Third, prizes were voted and established to encourage daily practice in each worthwhile emotional concept. The boy or girl who could relate an adequate example collected a reward for his or her emotional control.

Fourth, time was set aside once a week for depicting some of the emotional premises and concepts we had discussed. To illustrate, Jim and Danny would act out the premise that arguments usually start by telling someone he is wrong. The rest of the class would try to guess which premise was involved. Each correct answer earned X number of dollars. My class begged for the opportunity to play this type of charades each week.

Using this technique, emotional control and mental maturity came to my students much sooner than I believed possible. Naturally, I felt such a program at school should have a carryover in the home. When my parents began to express their pleasure, I was sure I was right. Yet, in spite of all of these favorable signs, I still wasn't completely convinced that the system was really responsible for most of these advances. Numerous teachers, and a few parents, insisted that it was my personality. Their opinions, I realized, came from the long established and widely accepted interpersonal relations theory, which establishes the teacher as the fountain of everything. If I hadn't personally witnessed the system at work, I might have agreed, especially when it was the most egotistical thing to do.

The enthusiastic ravings of parents continued so I decided to investigate further. A home visit seemed in order. This would shed more light on the system's accomplishments—or mine. A determination in favor of the system was very important, for methods can be taught, but personality traits seldom can. Perhaps I was on the verge of a discovery that could revolutionize classroom teaching. I tingled all over from excitement as I thought about it then. Elementary education could be changed from a one horsepower affair into thirty-five horsepower streamlined classrooms with universal adaptability.

Finally I came down to earth. At least a visit with the parents would reveal the extent of practical home application. If there was no carryover or retention outside of the classroom, I was wasting my time on the social part of the program and would have to concentrate on the academic portion almost exclusively.

CHAPTER 11
Home Visits
Parental Reactions to the System

I took my tape recorder and called on the parents of twenty-six of my pupils. I heard some amazing testimony for the system. Some statements were so startling and almost unbelievable that nothing less than actual quotations will do justice to the two-hour interview in every home. However, for the sake of brevity only a few presentations are offered here.

"Last year our son was not getting anything out of school with the established methods. This year he has changed completely." Such statements came from almost all, but when the conversation came down to specifics, I was flabbergasted.

"My son's grammar has improved tremendously. I teach school, but now he even comes home and corrects me. The discipline in your class, Mr. Harrison, has me toying with the idea that I can use your system with my pupils."

"This year my son has learned concepts far beyond that expected of an eleven year old. He has experienced them in the classroom."

"The child learns individual responsibility in this system. He has found that he can hurt only himself when he's fined or spends his money foolishly. And it's down in black and white where he can see this."

"He has learned leadership qualities such as patience and how to work with people instead of just telling them what to do."

"My child's outlook on life has been broadened. He now does things for himself first before calling on his parents for help."

"The child has discovered that minorities are more of a real people since he has had to work with them in the classroom in this system, and he has even had to ask them for some help sometimes, which is real good."

"In all previous years my child was the most hateful in school. They wanted to expell her from kindergarten and it's been the same since. But since entering the system she has changed completely. She now has a lot more friends, hates to miss school and is much more ambitious."

(This child made the following statement:) "I used to not like Negro kids and now I do because of the system. Also I now realize that when I cheat in the system I am cheating my friends and before I didn't care."

"We had all kinds of trouble last year with him at school and so he just gave up and wouldn't do anything. He couldn't understand it without help and so he wouldn't even try. We used to have big fights about this here at home but we haven't had this problem this year. I think this system is the greatest thing that's come along in education in the last twenty years."

"Our girl in the past was a selfish person. She couldn't get along with her classmates. But this year, she has learned to accept people for what they are and not who they are or what they can do for her. And she doesn't come home anymore and tell us how dumb some of her classmates act, or even how she made the highest score in the class. She used to enjoy telling us how she made some of her friends unhappy, and this year I haven't heard anything about this."

"The system is like real life," one of my students explained to his parents. "If you earn the money, you can go on the trips you like, and if you don't work you can't. This system allows you to move [academically] twice as fast as any other I've been in."

"Before, my boy would do only just what he had to. Now we have to force him to stop doing his homework and go to bed. He even brings other children home and helps them with their homework."

"Last year he came home and dropped his books and out he went, no matter how much we screamed or hollered at him. Now it's like playing around with real money and he wants to do it. He feels he is working for something and he enjoys it." (The pupil's explanation for his reversed behavior follows.) "The reason I like it this year is that I get a lot more help in the groups."

(One pupil described her feelings very well with the following statement): "This year the smart kids in your group can help. Last year there was a big line at the teacher's desk and you had to wait about a half hour to get even one question answered. Now I can just raise my hand and the student teacher answers it right away."

"Even on the vacations our boy can't wait to get back to school. He used to be a very nervous child and even got sick [from tension] whenever he played in the ball games or the teacher corrected him. But this year he is more relaxed and we don't have the problem anymore."

"The big change is in her attitude. Now she wants to learn." (And this student had this to say:) "Last year I didn't have a chance to understand people like I do this year. Now I work in the groups without any choice as to classmates. To work and earn things now gives me a feeling I like."

(A Spanish-speaking parent glowed with praise:) "He used to come home and say he couldn't do the homework, that it was too hard. Now he never says this and is anxious to do his schoolwork. His friends can't even get him to come out and play before he is finished."

"This year there has been no question about whether or not he will make it, only how well he can make it. Our boy has a real problem attending public schools [the pupil was almost deaf] and this year has been a real joy for him to go."

"In previous years if she was sick she would stay in bed and take advantage of it. Now she wants to go to school when she should stay home with her illness."

(This statement came from a working mother without a spouse.)

"I appreciate the self-reliance the system builds since this is a necessity when she is left here alone with her younger brother and sister while I work."

"I'm happy my girl had this system because if she hadn't I don't think she could ever make it in junior high."

"He just loves the system. He won't miss a single day of school now."

(One of the brightest of my pupils summed up his feelings about the system with the following statement:) "I don't know why I like it—it's just fun. I like to be a teacher and work and watch my bank account rise."

The truly amazing thing that struck me after two months of interviewing parents was the lack of complaints. One parent voiced her objection that her son didn't seem to read at home as much this year, until I pointed out that he was probably spending more time in other subject areas needing improvement. At the end of the school year I phoned this concerned parent to report that the recent achievement tests her son took revealed an overall average academic increase of three years. The mother was elated.

The fact that the interviews were conducted with only the pupils and their parents from one classroom strengthened my conviction that it was the system and not just me. However, I realized that an impartial observer might reach other conclusions. The big question was, how could I find out for sure?

CHAPTER 12
Early Struggles
Introduction of the System to Others

After such glowing testimonials, the next step was to interest others and solicit their support. The most logical place to begin had to be in my own school district with its administrators. Surely I had sufficient evidence to warrant their investigation. Or did I? If the system was as good as I thought it was, wouldn't they come to me? The old adage of "a better mouse trap" never seemed to have more applicability. Yet, was I really any closer to an accurate determination of the question vital to the system's expansion—my methods or me? Shouldn't I procrastinate and accumulate more proof, one way or the other? It certainly couldn't do any harm and the time would allow me to comb a few more bugs from the program. Thus, I settled the question in my mind. I felt certain that to wait was the best course of action.

And so the years slipped by without serious complications or, to my great surprise, any interest being shown in the system by my superiors. Slowly I realized that the educational business was really not a business at all. It operated by an entirely different set of rules. Not only was the old mouse trap theory not applicable but its utilization was definitely taboo when it created waves and rocked anyone's boat. Anything that promoted the status quo was sought and retained. As one school administrator put it: "We need lots of smoke without any fire."

It took me a number of years to understand and appreciate the practicality of this nonsense, at least from the school administrator's viewpoint. It was rationalized as follows:

a. Anything new which actually accomplished something couldn't possibly please everyone and always displeased a few.

b. Past experience revealed that minorities yell the loudest, especially when they are hurt, while the majority is so apathetic that most advancements go unnoticed and unrewarded.

c. Therefore, the successful school administrator sought and implemented innovations (thus he looked good in the eyes of his public), which offered a lot of smoke and no fire. And the most *preferred* educational bandaid was engineered by any well known doctorate from a local university. (This provided authority to satisfy laymen.)

After viewing the fate of a few excellent innovations which did accomplish something after they had accidentally slipped by the administrator's scrutiny, I found myself, first, almost ready to sympathize with the "smoke and no fire" philosophy and, second, inclined to hide my own novel methods. If it wasn't a teacher, it was a parent who bitterly complained about a new technique. Even the children didn't seem to appreciate it if the innovation were completely foreign. So the old, the tried, and the true stayed. This angered no one and seemed to get the job done, especially when there were no comparisons to create dissatisfactions. The few hardy souls who realized what was happening were eventually overcome by the smoke. The pattern followed something like this in my school district:

"Come and see our educational innovations," urged administrators.

"But my Johnny still can't read, in spite of your new techniques!" exclaimed parents after a two-year trial of the worthless methods.

"This innovation takes more of my time than it's ever worth," chimed in a number of teachers.

"But nobody can do a good job without adequate funds for more teacher assistance and materials!" cried the distraught and sincere administrator.

And so the money came in ever-increasing amounts but with no visible improvement. Johnny graduated and still couldn't read. The parents, being ignorant of the "smoke and no fire" theory, and not understanding the highly technical field of education, gnashed their teeth and opened their pocketbooks wider. When no results were forthcoming, they still seemed to have faith in their good doctor of education, especially if the worthless medicine was sugarcoated another way. The public's ignorance and gullibility became unreal.

Occasionally, I observed that a school board could be pressured into firing the good doctor. But then, lo and behold, everybody discovered that his replacement came from the same mold with the same basic procedure—smoke and no fire.

Finally the taxpaying parents became so incensed and disgusted that they fired the school board. With their newly-elected board members, the cycle was ready to start all over again.

So as the years passed I watched the taxpayers continue to shell out for one-horsepower education. The few voices shouting for change were labeled as cranks, or even worse if they had a practical remedy to offer, which was *not* the case in most instances. All who seemed to have a workable remedy were quickly silenced lest they rock someone's boat with their waves.

After a number of years spent as an observer and performer in such an educational circus, I knew that my system, no matter how successful, would die on the pedagogical vine before it was ever picked for sampling. If I were to get anyone to look at it, the effort would have to come from me alone. But at this point I always ended up asking myself, did I really want them to take a look?

Fortunately, I was not harassed inside my classroom during this period. In fact, I was ignored. For this, I was truly thankful, considering that my administrators possessed the power to eliminate the system whenever they chose. As I review all previous factors now, it does seem amazing that I had strength enough to proceed with anything more than my own private use of my unique methods. But I did. I gradually began to talk about some of my fantastic results, particularly in the areas of student self-discipline and self-motivation. I even discussed my classroom's high achievement test, which is normally taboo.

Some district administrators yawned and patted me on the back. "You're doing a great job, Al. Keep up the good work!" (My own principal always offered encouragement and meant it, but also found himself an outcast for his efforts.)

"But it's the system!" I argued. "Let me explain how it works."

If I had stuck my listener with a pin, he couldn't have seemed more alarmed. There were a dozen reasons, suddenly, why he had to be elsewhere.

"Sorry Al! Catch you next time! Gotta run!" were the stock excuses. Finally I brought up the subject just to see what anyone would say.

Occasionally, I found a kindly teacher who listened out of courtesy until he had the opportunity to explain his own "interpersonal relations" philosophy. "Yes, Al!" my colleague chided me. "It's a fine system, but so are most teacher's. Instructors have methods which are personal to them, just as yours are to you. No, Al! It's you that's so good and not the system." I heard this so often I wanted to scream in frustration. It accomplished little to argue with them, and my efforts only served to entrench opinions. Finally I gave up in disgust. Except to a few staunch friends who truly appreciated what I was trying to accomplish, I said little more than "good morning!"

My nature being what it is, I could stand this silence for only a limited period of time. Something as good as the system just had to be displayed. But how, when nobody would listen? The real source of my difficulties, I imagined then, lay in the size of the system. It was always the vastness that defeated me. I couldn't possibly explain how it worked in the few minutes available to my listener. Nothing less than a book would adequately cover the subject, and even then it would be adequate only as a description, and not as a teaching guide. Thus I set about becoming an author.

I read every instructional book I could find on the subject of writing until I realized that the task might be beyond my capabilities. But challenge has always been my bread and butter. I forced myself to continue with the self-education. Slowly and painfully I progressed, writing in the evening and in spare moments. The book gradually grew, page by page, but try as I would, I couldn't seem to keep my frustrations out of it. This was vital to objective reading, but all I could do *was* try.

Approximately half way through the book the blow fell. The district administrators decided that I had been at Sunnydale too long. Mono Elementary needed a sixth grade teacher for the start of the fall term and I would be it.

Dear God! I thought. What would happen to the system and me now? Mr. Brown, an educator with the district for many many years, would be my new principal. Mr. Turner's wonderful support and protection would be no more, and what was worse, this was my tenure year in which I would achieve permanent status in the district. The administrators had timed it perfectly. Either this next year I shaped up or they shipped me out of the district. The message was clear.

Well, I was a big boy now, maybe I could stand on my own two feet. Maybe, nothing! I had to! There was at least one pillar of support upon which I felt that I could rely—my former pupils' parents. I had heard by way of the grapevine that many words of praise had been spoken in my behalf to administrators and school board members. Perhaps with some of the community's most influential citizens singing my praise, it would be tough to fire me without good cause. And I didn't propose to give them any cause.

I reported for work the first of September, expecting the worst, but not really fearful. The ax fell on the third day in the teacher's lounge. Mr. Brown asked me into his office for a short discussion on my unique teaching methods.

"I know all about the system you use, Al." Mr. Brown's face was serious and I knew he wasn't kidding, but for the life of me I couldn't imagine how he knew, since he had never been one of the administrators I had badgered previously with the system. "Now, I've had orders to put a stop to this system of reward and punishment you use or, at least, you are going to have to tone the program down. You can start by calling those academic dollars you give by another name, such as points or credits. It's just too commercial to have in the classroom."

"Whoa! Back up!" I exclaimed. "If what you are saying is that you want me to get rid of the system, you're just whistling in the dark. Rather than go back to teaching conventionally, I'll quit right now, or you can fire me for insubordination. Conventional instruction is a thought too painful to contemplate.

"Now, on the other hand," I continued, replacing my worried frown with a friendly smile, "if you have some minor objections, I'll be glad to make the changes."

Either my smile or my firm attitude squeezed just a trace of friendliness from my opponent, which showed in his voice. "Well, no need to get angry about it, Al!"

"Okay!" I replied, "I'll call them points instead of dollars."

It took only two weeks to realize that my round-one victory had been just a preliminary to the main event. I was informed that the after-school student trips might be objectionable. I made a special trip to the superintendent's office to solicit his permission for the trips. After extensive discussion he consented so long as my automobile carried sufficient insurance for the protection of my pupils. He accepted three hundred thousand dollars as a minimum figure. I left his office filled with hope and anxious to impart this news to Mr. Brown the next day.

Mr. Brown threw up his hands in disgust upon hearing the decision. As a result, for the rest of the year, I was pretty well ignored, outside of routine matters. We both kept our silent agreement to stay out of each other's hair, until I made the mistake of answering questions about the system asked by a few of the school's new teachers. One of the veteran instructors jealously complained that I was leading the new lambs astray and I was called into the office. "You are to keep your methods to yourself, from now on!" I was informed in very blunt tones. The white silk gloves had been discarded in favor of those worn in the ring. No more under-the-table stuff. Evidently it was official warfare if I stepped beyond the self-utilization stage.

A challenge has always intrigued me and I tingled with the thought of accepting this one. But still, as an amateur in the educational field, I couldn't begin to visualize what it was I faced. If I had known then what I know now, I'm not certain what action I would have taken. But one thing I do know now: if my antagonists had possessed that ability to see into the future, they would have taken the strongest action possible against me then. My tenure would certainly have been refused, which is tantamount to a dismissal in the teaching profession. As it was, developments were almost that bad.

Toward the end of the school year most school districts require that their administrators render an efficiency report on their teachers. This report describes, in a very general way, how proficient each instructor is. Seldom do such evaluations receive much more than a glance from the superintendent before being filed in the usual cobweb-filled drawer which is opened only at promotion time. However, the one exception to this callous procedure comes at tenure time. Once permanent status is given, firing a teacher is difficult indeed. Therefore, if so much as a shadow of a doubt exists concerning the teacher's future performance, his tenure is refused and he frequently finds he is barred from teaching elsewhere for this same reason.

During my tour of duty with the Air Force, I earned a small pension for a nervous stomach. This school year I had been earning it all over again. My nervous system dumped gallons of acid on what little food I ate every day, as the time for tenure reports drew near. When the dreaded day arrived, I was called in to Mr. Brown's office and asked to sign the following tenure report:

> Al has done a very good job using his method of approach in the classroom. The boys and girls like him, also parents. He has everything worked out whereby pupils direct with a merit reward and punishment type learning situation. I see very little room for growth or change using this system. Al has requested that he be transferred to another school next year. I agree such a change is needed both for Al and myself. We are not in agreement with Al's techniques and methods in the classroom therefore a change seems to be the answer. I believe Al can do a good job and forget his reward type teaching. I have tried to get him to use a regular or typical approach without results. He has been notified that his methods are not approved here. I recommend that he be transferred and given direction by our curriculum director and superintendent.

At first I refused to sign until it was explained that my signature didn't mean agreement, but instead, merely understanding. I signed.

I held my breath for over a month, awaiting my dismissal. During this trying period a veteran instructor continually urged me to mend my ways. "Why don't you give in, Al?" he said about twice every day. "Just think how pleasant life could be. Teach conventionally and draw your pay check once a month like I do instead of fighting for it." I never could determine whether this individual was envious of the system's superior classroom results, as some of his previous actions had indicated, or if he truly felt sorry for me. Before I had an adequate opportunity to find out, my superiors made their decision on the much more important tenure question.

I was offered a contract for the following school year. This, I learned, was tantamount to granting tenure. No explanation, no comment and no message, but I had won. I was elated and my stomach cramps became a mere sour stomach. Emboldened by this success I went a step further and again requested a transfer back to my old principal, Mr. Turner. To my complete surprise it was granted. Evidently my presence hadn't improved poor Mr. Brown's digestion either.

After that experience, I knew the system's only salvation lay in a book detailing my techniques. It required all of that summer vacation to complete the manuscript. The last chapter contained comments and criticisms, and couldn't be included until they were rendered by my district's administrators and teachers. At the time, it seemed like an excellent way to solicit local attention.

I supplied carbon copies of the manuscript to selected reviewers and received their written statements in about a month. But strangely, no one had enough interest to visit my classroom. I thanked them for a splendid critique and incorporated their statements into the last chapter of the book. I admit that I was more than a little disappointed in their apathy but consoled myself with the thought that there were other districts than mine. Most prophets become outcasts in their own territory.

At least I then felt that I had the tool necessary for disseminating the system. Even if the manuscript wasn't written well, I had something which, I hoped, had consolidated my thoughts into an understandable whole. Also, what did it matter if some of my frustrations had escaped into the printed page? Perhaps sympathy might move the reader to at least take a deeper look. But how naive I was. As a newborn writer I was to discover that I knew nothing about anything.

The next step took me to the *Writer's Market,* which is a book containing what its title indicates. I was staggered and bewildered by the large number available. An agent seemed like the thing to have. To such an individual, placement of the manuscript would be easy.

With this thought in mind, I wrote to a very busy and famous local author, Erle Stanley Gardner. As could be expected, no reply arrived. Finally I phoned his home and reached his secretary who graciously listened long enough to ask Mr. Gardner to drop me a line. A few days later I received his treasured reply. But sadly, it didn't reveal much more than I already knew: agents accept known authors only. I was back where I started.

Determined to make one last attempt, I used a national writer's magazine to find an agent who advertised for unpublished writers and then fired off my manuscript to him. Back came a reply, "Fifty dollars, please, for the evaluation." I sent the money immediately.

I received an ego-smashing evaluation with my manuscript about a month later. It was two months before I recovered and even longer before I could think of this agent's name with anything but hate.

The evaluation letter went far beyond anything I could previously imagine to boldly state that "the dangers in my teaching methods were not so great that they could not be cancelled by devoted teachers on a higher level." Other statements were: "Not to learn English grammar, composition, syntax, disqualifies you to speak broadly on the subject of education." "By striving to be the personality teacher in your prose, by stressing always the immediate, the pragmatic, you undermine respect in your methods as well as your curriculum." And "No, be assured that this project has no legitimate market sale, Mr. Harrison, because it doesn't deserve one. Motivation is one thing, but not the end-all of education. It is of quite secondary nature—indispensable, but an adjunct, an accessory. All that counts is the training of the young mind in proper thinking techniques, rather than cramming it with rote information."

I seethed inside. But as some wise man said, time heals all, and it did me. Slowly I realized that just such a frank and candid review was what I needed. Actually this agent had done me a great service with his sharp knife, and now I had to do some cutting myself. Hadn't I admitted to allowing my frustrations to creep into print? Well, if it took a literary ax to chop them out, so be it. After all, what good was the written word which was never read? It was back to the old typewriter.

I spent the spare moments of the next six months completely rewriting the manuscript. As I wrote I began to realize just how chauvinistic and belligerent my previous messages might seem. Again, naively, I thought that this might account for my administrators' disinterest. Just to make sure, I rewrote the whole book for the third time.

Finally I felt I was ready, except for one hang up—my book had a split personality. It was slanted toward the general reader yet it contained specific instructions to the teacher for implementing the system. The instructor was forced to wade through pages to get the meat of the system, and the ordinary citizen was forced to absorb my accurate system details.

Well there was no help for it now, I thought. The book would have to stand or fall on its own. I had other promotional measures in mind and I couldn't spend any more time writing. And besides, by then I was sick of the typewritten word. Even my students sensed this inside the classroom. I definitely needed a rest or at least a diversion.

I mailed over thirty-five query letters to the major book publishers without success. Finally, Prentice-Hall asked to see the manuscript and I sent it on its way. They kept it for about four months and my spirits soared until it was returned with a rejection slip.

Next I mailed it to Dorrance & Company. The very short letter they sent put me on cloud nine. They liked it with "a few minor revisions." Then it rained on cloud nine. A letter came quoting prices necessary for the book's publication. I had failed to notice that Dorrance was a subsidy publisher. And so it went for the next few months.

Finally I sent the manuscript to the Utah Press in Salt Lake City, which is the official publishing organ for the Mormon Church. The editor liked the book and the philosophy it contained so much that he came to Riverside to see the system in action. He solicited comments on the book from two reviewers. The first appeared to be a teacher of sociology and the other of psychology. They tore into the book's philosophy like a starved lion at a water hole. Despite his reviewers' adverse opinions, the editor evidently still liked the book and its philosophy because he kept the manuscript over four years before having his assistant return it to me without comment. I suspect he had as much difficulty with his superiors' decisions and opinions as I did with mine. So much for my delving into authorship. Needless to say, I thought long and strong before beginning this narrative. But at least no one will be able to say that I haven't tried.

Actually my escapades in the literary field were really only a small part of my struggles to disseminate the system. I wrote to the big non-profit foundations seeking whatever assistance they might care to give.

Specifically I requested measurements of my fantastic results, both social and academic, which I knew were there. Rather than record every reply, I shall let only a few of the largest speak for all thirty-three.

I am sorry to say that the Ford Foundation is not in a position to help you in the ways you suggested. Our staff is a small one and we have found it necessary to adopt a policy of not accepting manuscripts for appraisal. Nor are we prepared at this time to introduce or promote your system. —Ford Foundation

Much to my regret I am compelled to inform you that what you have in mind in the way of a pilot program in education is wholly outside the general concerns of the Sloan Foundation.
—Alfred P. Sloan Foundation

We do not advocate specific teaching methods and we have a firm policy against subsidizing the publication of manuscripts, with the occasional exception of research which results from our grants.
—Carnegie Corporation of New York

[W]e are not in a financial position to provide assistance. This is due to the fact that we have heavy commitments to ongoing projects in both science and education. —Charles F. Kettering Foundation

Unfortunately, we cannot help as the interest of our trustees lies in a different area. —Vincent Astor Foundation

The point in your last paragraph is well made. I'm afraid foundations have spent an unreasonably large share of their funds at the higher levels of education. We have long been interested in private education at the primary and secondary levels, but have restricted support for such schools to Marion County, Indiana. As I say, we have done practically nothing in public schools, for we have preferred to help schools which cannot tap into tax sources of support. —Lilly Endowment, Inc.

As I wrote you recently, I have circulated your manuscript among some of the key people in the economic education movement in order to assure that its potential would be given thorough consideration by influential professionals in the field. I regret to have to report to you that all have failed to see anything significantly new or promising in your particular approach. I am, therefore, returning your material with my appreciation for your courtesy in letting me see it and my regrets that my efforts were not more productive and helpful.
—Calvin K. Kazanjian Economics Foundation, Inc.

The rejections from the foundations seemed to center on two facts: I had no acceptable personal credentials or recommendations, and neither did my system. I faced the age-old frustration of every innovator: "Show us results and we'll listen." But how can you show results unless someone somewhere first listens?

Being a nobody in education, I was probably being presumptuous even to think about asking for assistance from busy foundations. They had other pressing business (as they repeatedly told me in their letters) with much more assurances of success.

For the next source of assistance I sought the wealthy. Surely these were the people with the most to lose from a sick society. Such influential persons would hear my cries for help with open ears and maybe open pocketbooks. Didn't many multimillionaires also sit on the board of directors for foundations?

But I forgot one logical and very important point in my assumption. I faced hardheaded businessmen who demanded even more facts and figures than the foundations if they were to risk their fortunes and reputations on any such venture in the field of education.

What meager facts and information I possessed came as a result of my own efforts as a single classroom instructor. Naturally, this was insufficient for their needs and they sought opinions and recommendations from the very people most likely to be opposed to what I was trying to accomplish—the school administrators and education professors. It isn't hard to guess what these worthy sources suggested any more than it was when the foundations sought their recommendations. Nevertheless, a few quoted replies from the sixty wealthy men I queried will say what needs to be said.

> I have sent your letter of October 27 describing the Harrison System to Dr. M. L. Frankel, President of the Joint Council on Economic Education. This group has long had a splendid program of teaching economics in the schools, and it has had my steady support for many years. I think it is one of the most effective organizations of its kind in the country.
> —Thomas B. McCabe
> (of the Scott Paper Company)

> Mr. Mellon has referred your letter of July 22nd to me for reply. I regret to advise you that, because of his many existing commitments in fields of his own interest, he cannot take an interest in your educational system. I am returning the synopsis you enclosed, together with the recorded tape, in case you have additional use for them.
> —Thomas H. Beddall, Jr.
> Assistant to Paul Mellon

I am returning herewith the tape forwarded with your letter of July 22. Because I do not feel myself an expert in the evaluation of teaching systems, I asked for a review of your proposals by experienced educators who have produced demonstrated results in the motivation to and learning of children. It was their opinion that you have developed the germ of a good idea but that it could not be considered a "cure-all" in the educational field as helpful as this would be. Nevertheless, we certainly want to extend our best wishes to you for your continued interest in education and developments that will be helpful to young children.

—Erik Jonsson
(of Dallas, Texas)

Your letter of July 22, addressed to Mr. J. Howard Pew, has been referred to us for attention. We administer the affairs of the Pew Memorial Trust as its corporate trustee. This Trust was established many years ago by Mr. Pew and other members of his family. Under our present operating policies, our participation in the educational program is normally limited to the collegiate level and we cannot, therefore, help in your project. We are sorry that we cannot be of assistance.

—Allyn R. Bell, Jr.
(of the Glennmede Trust Company)

I have received your letter of July 24th addressed to me at Huntington and the sample tape and I don't know what action you would like to have me take. I am active in the audio-visual business through the Industrial Products Div. of Fairchild Camera & Instrument Corp., through Conrac Corp., and through IBM. I couldn't agree with you more about the slowness with which we adopt modern teaching methods and I think it is solely because there is much local authority in our school system. There is no question that the Japanese are way ahead of us.

Conrac Corp. has just purchased a company in Germany who are the main manufacturer and distributor of educational systems there and Conrac is not even bothering to bring the German system to this country, because of the difficulty in selling it here.

Therefore, I'd like to have you let me know just what action you would like to have me take that could be specific. The desired action is probably going to be to change our whole educational approach but I have to tell you now that I can't take on the job.

—Sherman Fairchild
(of Dynar Corporation)

Mr. Norris asked me to review the material which you forwarded to him. We have spent some time considering the educational approach you outlined and reviewing the magnetic tape which you kindly lent us and which we have enclosed.

There is no question that the educational approach outlined is basically attractive, but, at the same time, we feel that it is also as one sided as you obviously feel the current methods have become. As a corporation, we are very much aware of the perpetuation of certain social problems which, although not intended, are not solvable without specific social actions taking place inside our free enterprise system. Consequently, our complete support of the free enterprise system is tempered to the extent that it requires sufficient modifications to include those which have been excluded from its benefits. An educational system that gets all of these points across would be ideal in our minds. We frankly don't feel that you have found the necessary educational balance that is needed. We appreciate very much you sharing your thoughts on this with us and the opportunity to comment on it.

—Norbert R. Berg
(of Control Data Corporation)

Your letter of October 27th addressed to Mr. Allan Kirby has been received here in his office. Mr. Kirby has been seriously ill for the last two-and-a-half years and is unable to consider your program or to reply to your letter.

I have taken the liberty of reading the material which you sent and have done so with much interest.

It is not out of the question that I might provide you with modest financial support if convinced of an all over superiority for your method of teaching. It is easy to be impressed with the desirability of emphasis on the capitalistic approach in our schools to combat the all too prevalent socialistic approach. But, your emphasis on surrounding the students with capitalism at work must take a great deal of time away from the pursuit of the conventional, non-controversial, academic subjects.

It seems to me as though, if your system is deserving of substantial financial support from people who are not in a position objectively to judge its academic merits, it must first have support on at least an experimental basis from nationally known educators. At such time as you can demonstrate such support I should be glad to hear further from you.

—F. M. Kirby
(of Morristown, New Jersey)

My head being as hard as those of the business tycoons I wanted to interest, it never occurred to me to give up. If no one was interested in examining the system on its own merits, perhaps I could induce some prestigious individual to lend his endorsement to the philosophy embodied in my methods.

I sent out numerous letters of appeal to such famous personalities as Bob Hope, John Wayne, Senator (then Representative) John Tunny, and even Ex-President and General Dwight Eisenhower, to name only a few. Perhaps not quite typical of the replies received was the curt message from Dr. Max Rafferty, at that time state superintendent of California education, which I shall quote verbatim:

> Thank you for your letter of October 5.
>
> I appreciate your interest in writing to me, and I read the enclosed synopsis with great interest. Unfortunately, I cannot review book manuscripts for two reasons: (1) I would be swamped with hundreds of them, and (2) I'm not in the publishing business.
>
> I advise you to submit your manuscript to some of the leading publishing houses.
>
> Cordially,
> Max Rafferty

I didn't in any way feel resentful of the apathetic answers. By now I was grateful for any reply. After all, I realized that these were very busy personages who couldn't really spare valuable time to investigate every plea for assistance, no matter how worthy it might seem.

But it wasn't in my nature to give up this easily. With the help of Rampart College, I sent my oldest son, Frank, on a personal visit to John Wayne. He cornered the old free enterpriser at his home in Newport Beach, California, but the results were still the same. I had a five minute visit (that's all he could spare) with Representative Tunny. He didn't see how he could help me and insisted that I should talk to the local school administrators. I thanked him and departed.

Only one of the VIPs I contacted expressed enthusiasm. Lt. General William Martin, USAF Retired, former commander of the 15th Air Force, came to my home to express his considerable interest. He even offered the services of his friend, an artist and personal relations expert. But nothing developed beyond the discussion stage. I hadn't the necessary finances to support much of an undertaking and no one else seemed interested.

Still my determination knew no bounds. I wrote to President Lyndon B. Johnson. He referred my letter to the Office of Education, and I received a reply from the department in charge of innovations and new projects. This letter outlined the extensive requirements for a federally-financed education project. So what if the requirements seemed impossible? I thought. At least this was a start. The impossible was getting to be routine and never had I been this close to a taste of success. But little did I know.

I busied myself in obtaining fifty copies of this and ten carbons of that. I even personally wrote the twenty- or thirty-page project report that frequently takes experts months to compile with its financial estimates and personnel requirements. Finally everything seemed in readiness except for the major requirements—I needed a school district which would accept a federal grant for the purpose of experimenting with the system. In fact the Office of Education had even assigned a project number to my program. I spent the next two or three months trying to persuade my district administrators to investigate this government proposal. It required only an administrative commitment to take a look and be paid for doing so. I wasted my time; no one was interested.

That was the last straw as far as I was concerned. But my sense of loyalty to my district forced me to try one more source of assistance—my local school board. I personally visited all five board members to explain in detail and answer questions about the system. Further, I played the tape recording of my parent's comments and mentioned the possibilities available with a federally-financed project. All of the members were politely interested and one, the chairman of the board, offered to provide an official hearing on the system before the board. I agreed with alacrity. But it took about a year before the presentation could be scheduled.

Meanwhile I decided that if my own school district was in no hurry to examine the system, perhaps others might. I began contacting numerous local teachers associations. Their presidents were either apathetic or frightened. Where were my endorsements and what proof did I possess? Facts and figures were demanded. Once again I faced the same brick wall. I even made a trip to the central office of the associations with the hope of interesting them. My son, Frank, helped me, and both of us made no progress whatsoever.

Next I visited some private schools, and the central office of the association to which many belonged. The "sorry, not interested!" always punctuated the end of the interview until I almost wished that just once the very polite school director would get angry in the beginning and throw me out, and save both of us a lot of time. Well, there were only two more sources to explore and I could logically expect both to be even less receptive than the rest. But being as persistent as I am, I launched an information attack upon the colleges.

I wrote and spoke to a number of education professors about the possibility of appearing before their students with a system presentation. Nothing developed until a friend of mine managed to have me invited to an education class he was taking in San Bernardino. That was my first and last appearance as an unsolicited guest. The socialistically-oriented students of that particular class actually seemed offended. Didn't elementary school pupils love to learn just for the sheer joy of it? Why would they need to be bribed? I backed out of that classroom as gracefully as possible after inadvertently hitting some of education's sacred cows in the head with an ax.

After that I turned my attention to the hundreds of school districts located throughout Southern California. My son, Frank, also helped me in this endeavor since he was well versed in the system and considerably more adroit in its presentation. Frank contacted most of the San Diego County school districts and the county superintendent of schools there. I spent my time similarly in Riverside, San Bernardino, Orange and Los Angeles Counties. The top-echelon administrators listened politely as I played the tape of my parents' comments and explained the system's operations. They accepted my written material for study, and all, except one whom I couldn't catch, replied in their best negative prose. I was accorded similar treatment by the district superintendents, whenever I managed to get by the ever-watchful and efficient personal secretary, which wasn't often. For these administrators, I left a miniature copy of the tape and the written material. Answers, when I received them at all, were always negative.

A few district superintendents accorded me the privilege of an extensive interview. I did see a glimmer of interest on the first contact but upon returning for further discussion it had disappeared. The reason for this never dawned until my own county superintendent refused to visit my classroom after promising that he would. When pressed for a reason, he finally admitted to an objection voiced by my own district's superintendent. This convinced me of the folly of what I was doing. As fast as I could interest an administrator, my own would turn him off. The percentages for success, under such an arrangement, were slim indeed.

Through strenuous persuasive efforts, Frank managed to induce thirteen top administrators from a San Diego area school district to travel over a hundred miles for the purpose of seeing the system in action. At the time, they seemed quite impressed but I never received any communication to that effect. The reason now was obvious, at least to me. Evidently they made the mistake of phoning my district administrators after their visit rather than before. Otherwise they might have saved themselves the trip.

A number of years before I began hunting for administrators I managed to teach the system's fundamentals to a very good friend and a fellow fifth grade instructor, Edward Lion. He was very innovative and interested in anything new. His own classroom contained unique techniques which, in many ways, were superior to my own. But not being static, he sought change for the sheer joy of it.

Ed Lion quizzed me about system methods while we were spectators at some of the local football games. Gradually he had his own system operating, patterned after mine. Naturally this drew the displeasure of our district administrators. Nevertheless he continued to use the system, in defiance of his superiors, and still uses it as of this writing with great success.

About three years after Lion started his system another colleague, Jim Pecan, read my manuscript and became so excited he began the full program inside his sixth grade classroom. He told me later that his original inducement came from his personal observation of the system's success inside my classroom which was located next door to his own.

"I just couldn't stand your pupils always academically trouncing mine," he said.

Jim's room and mine competed in spell-downs, vocabulary games, and various other academic contests. He drove his students with unrelenting force trying to win. But neither his disciplinary measures nor his motivational techniques seemed to make any difference; he always lost the academic contest. Being a very competitive fellow, he could stand only so much of that treatment. He asked for my secret and I gave him the manuscript to read.

It took Jim about two months to inaugurate most of the system inside his classroom but he still didn't give the manuscript back until another three months had passed. Unknown to me, he had loaned it to Jan Sweet, a kindergarten teacher in our school district who adapted the system to her own needs. Naturally, she geared everything downward and operated with maximum simplicity. Very soon she too was singing the system's praises.

Now there were four system teachers in the Mono School District, much to the consternation of its administrators. Pressure was applied to the weakest of our number. Inasmuch as Jan was the newest in the district and therefore more vulnerable, she was selected. It logically followed that she would be the easiest to dissuade, but the administrators had failed to consider her tremendous spirit and stamina. Jan found herself an outcast at her school and at complete odds with her principal, where things previously had been harmonious. She fought back the only way she could, by improving the performance inside her classroom.

Jan's pupils zoomed to the top of the academic achievement chart and the behavior of her students became the talk of the whole school. Naturally, parents were more than pleased and tried to express their gratitude and appreciation to Jan's administrators. This seemed only to further infuriate her superiors and it served to increase the pressure. Jan's performance report ratings dropped to the bottom, despite demonstrated outstanding achievement in both academic and social areas. Finally such tactics had her in tears and she requested a transfer to another elementary school in the district. Very reluctantly it was approved.

The administrative pressure stayed on. It made little difference *where* she taught, it was the *way* she taught. The harassment continued throughout the next school year. She received disgracefully low performance reports; her classroom was loaded with known discipline and academic problems; and finally, when she still stubbornly stuck with the system, her administrators refused to properly support her decisions concerning pupils and parents.

I helped Jan where I could by relating her sad plight to the school board members. Fortunately for Jan they acted in time to dissuade further obvious administrative pressures. She earned her tenure, and after transferring once more, has settled down to enjoy the system in her room exclusively. After such abuse she claims she isn't interested in stirring up more by trying to introduce any of her colleagues to the merits of the system. But she also declares that she wouldn't go back to teaching conventionally for a million dollars.

The administrators won at least a partial victory: they succeeded in preventing widespread acceptance and use of the system. But they were due for a surprise.

CHAPTER 13
Some Successes
Disseminating the System

About the same time that Jan was learning the system, I embarked upon a program for expansion. If my system was ever going to survive administrative attacks, many more instructors would need to use it. I knew there was safety in numbers. But how to go about accomplishing this was another matter. With most of the administrators in Southern California disinterested or antagonistic, I couldn't expect much chance of success outside of my own school district. The problem seemed insolvable.

Inasmuch as my district was the only one open to me, it followed that here I had to start, despite the fact that it was also the center of my opposition. At least here I was known and I definitely had some parental support, not to mention a tiny core of system teachers. That was much more than I had elsewhere. And so began the beginning of the end.

I designed and duplicated an invitation to all of the Mono teachers and then hand-carried each notice to every school in the district. All instructors were invited to the junior high school library for a practical explanation of how they could achieve self-motivation and self-discipline with their pupils.

The bait was juicy indeed and should have drawn most of the district's instructors in spite of administrative opposition. If anyone but I had been presenting the information, all of the district's two hundred teachers would have been there. As it was, approximately thirty came and listened for an hour. At the end of the meeting twenty-two of the thirty signed for my free fifteen-hour course. I was elated. Here was fantastic progress in my own backyard and under the very noses of the enemy. And to top everything off one of the signatures was an administrator's, a minor one who evidently had not yet received the warning. But my elation was premature. The next day I was asked to strike the administrator's name from my list. And that was only the beginning. Before the administrators had finished with my recruits, the total was whittled to twelve.

I developed an outline for teaching the system and we met in my classroom at the junior high school. (The year before I had been transferred to the junior high along with all of the sixth graders from Sunnydale Elementary.) The course I taught my new recruits consumed two hours twice a week for a period of three and a half weeks.

At that time I discovered a very effective recruitment technique, the reverse psychology principle, which had exciting applicability for the system. The new recruit was warned from the beginning of the system's self-satisfaction trap. I told the teachers that they implemented the system at their own risk. Once inaugurated, neither the teacher nor her pupils would ever again be satisfied with ordinary methods. This was a fact that I had observed from the three people now using the system. Naturally, that created a challenge hard to resist and induced some to at least try it and see. Thus, I had a 95 percent acceptance rate from the more than a hundred who were eventually taught in Southern California.

Also, during this period, I revived my badgering of top administrators in my district. For a number of years, I had maintained that much larger classes could be taught with the system. "Give me a larger class and I'll show you," I had said. This, so I thought at the time, would prove the system's value beyond any doubt. But I failed to reckon with administrative thinking in regards to power structures. More teachers mean larger empires, and more children per teacher will shrink empires. It took me awhile to realize this.

But I received the surprise of my life when I returned to schoolteaching in the fall. My request had been approved and I was to have approximately forty-five pupils instead of the customary thirty to thirty-five. My class was to be built from the rejects of my sixth grade colleagues. But so many rejects were found, and so many pupil requests for transfer were made, that my class size rose to fifty-seven (I averaged about fifty-five for the school year).

At first I couldn't understand my administrators' change of heart. Had I really won? And, if so, were they now going to give the system a fair examination? Now that I have more facts upon which I can base an opinion, I am convinced that no charity prompted my administrators' actions. The school district had everything to gain and nothing to lose, financially and otherwise. The district saved a teacher's salary for the extra children I taught, but perhaps of more importance to the administrators was the opportunity to eliminate that hated system of mine. Their thinking probably went something like this: What teacher anywhere can double his class size with undesirables, double the average academic achievement and promote social growth in his pupils all at the same time? The administrators felt certain that they had me and the system at last. Within three months, they thought, I would be hollering Uncle. But they had another thought coming, as time would prove.

Next, I sought and received permission from my local teachers association to present an official program on the system to my colleagues. This presentation would be in the nature of endorsements from the district's twelve system teachers rather than the usual rehash of the system's operation. Here at last, or so I thought, I was going to have some factual substantiation and recognition for the merits of the system besides my own. But again, it wasn't going to come that easily.

With this renewed recruitment drive by me the administrators had stepped up their pressure against system teachers. Some of my new recruits had been frightened at the prospect of open warfare with their superiors. A few had backed out of the system entirely but the majority remained committed so that I was not forced to send a letter of retraction to all of the invited teachers associations in Riverside and San Bernardino Counties. However my district did manage to schedule a teacher's inservice workshop for salary credit at exactly the same time and place as my system presentation. This very effectively eliminated many of my local colleagues.

When the day finally arrived, seven of my system teachers stood before an audience of about 200 and related how the methods had helped them in the classroom. I made a tape recording of their statements, and I have selected passages which will give the most information with the least redundance.

A kindergarten teacher: "I innovated on the system for kindergarten [everything is scaled down]. I use chips, which are more tangible for this grade level. The chips become valuable and the children learn to count right away. The child even knows the value of the chip on the floor which is not rightfully his. He also comes to understand that if he throws sand on the playground, and perhaps becomes bankrupt, he must work hard to earn his way out before playtime comes again.

"After auction time, my high achievers find that their money has been almost completely spent and they have to start building their bank of chips all over again. This affords my low achievers the chance to succeed at the next auction or at least eventually. This system affords most children in the room an opportunity to be successful."

A fifth grade teacher: "Today we teach a meaningless socialism in the classroom and then we wonder why kids who graduate don't know how to face life. We don't teach self-discipline; we have a dictatorship. This system allows the teacher to teach the American way of life—self-discipline. Without this one virtue, the police would be helpless and our nation ripe for totalitarianism. This system teaches the value of property, money, self-motivation, and many of the other concepts that are so important and yet never taught or experienced in the conventional classrooms.

"The ivory tower approach used in today's classrooms assumes that everybody is good and will do what is right, therefore, there is no need for locks on doors and such things. The system allows children to learn in the classroom from failure as well as successes. In fact failures are turned into successes.

"In my room, the children learn to operate their own government and succeed in self-control through experience. By using this system of reward, meaningful to children, teachers can eliminate the ivory tower philosophy where the teacher runs everything."

A fourth grade teacher: "This is the only comprehensive system available today for classroom motivation and control. It gives the top students opportunities to become leaders inside the classroom. The system also takes care of most of the bothersome details associated with classroom teaching, such as lost pencils, restroom trips and so forth. The child learns that he can't disturb the teacher, only himself."

A second grade teacher: "The parents become delighted as the children learn what life is like as an adult. After the experience inside the classroom my children never forget and I feel that it will be useful throughout their lives. This system also gives more opportunity to the teacher to foster creativity, and initiative."

An eighth grade junior high teacher: "The college taught me to teach the whole child with individualized instruction but this was impossible for me to do with thirty children in the classroom. The system allows you to do this through the services of your children. The children become motivated and interested.

"The system helps me be consistent, which too few teachers are today. I can't play favorites anymore. I have to fine them when they misbehave.

"I learned many new things about my children whenever I took them on trips. Some teachers auction off real money instead of taking pupils on recreational trips, but I think I prefer to spend more time with my students rather than less; this allows me to help them more.

"At last I have found that my pupils are trying to work with me rather than against me. This is a great joy rather than a day-to-day game of combat as it was in the past."

A seventh grade math teacher: "It is the best method to use with the low groups. These kids learn a lot more with this system."

A sixth grade teacher: "I was a former primary teacher who had very real fears about moving to the intermediate level, especially regarding discipline problems. Last year I found these fears to be well founded. I had a lot of trouble. Since I started to use the system most of my problems have disappeared. My parents are satisfied. My pupils are now motivated and even the boys work at tasks they wouldn't do before. My principal has indicated he is well satisfied this year since I started the system."

Much to my disappointment, nothing came from this presentation of system teachers' testimonials, except for the news release described later in this chapter. But such unconcern should have come as no surprise after witnessing so much previous apathy.

A year and a half before, when I had gone administrator-hunting outside of my own school district, I had failed to contact the Orange County superintendent of education. His busy schedule kept me from an appointment until about six months had gone by. Finally we got together. Dr. Robert Petersen read my manuscript (he even made a copy of it for himself) and listened to the tape of my parents with honest enthusiasm. Then he visited three of our system classrooms in Mono Valley (about seventy miles distant). He came not as an administrator but rather as a dedicated college instructor with pupils who might be interested in the system. This prevented any official hassle and any objection from my administrators.

What Dr. Peterson saw in our classrooms excited him even further. He invited me, and any other system teachers who cared to come, to his college classroom. Several system teachers presented the system to no less than three different classes of his, but with no appreciable advancement for the system. However, I was grateful for the attitude of interest his students did display.

This great man did more to encourage me than probably any other educator outside of my own family. We had long talks together and his sympathy was invaluable. But even as a friend and sympathizer, there was little he could do. I realized that any move to assist me in his official capacity as Orange County superintendent of education might very well be fatal to his political career and would most certainly destroy any effectiveness with his own administrators. To promote me or my system among educational empire-builders was to court disaster.

But my greatest source of assistance came not from any one person but rather from a concern long known for its adversity to the tax-supported school and for its dedication to causes of freedom and individualism. The *Santa Ana Register* is a truly great newspaper which says it as it is. From Mr. Hoiles, the publisher, and his editors, on down to Archie Shamblin, one of their crack reporters, I found all to be searchers for the truth and facts, regardless of the consequences. It made little difference that I had the awesome power of the education establishment against me. The personnel of this newspaper printed the facts as they found them and as no other newspaper had the courage to do, despite many requests from me.

Not only did the system get local headlines in the *Santa Ana Register* but the Associated Press picked up the story. After this, local radio became interested, and even national television tried for two weeks to contact me through my administrators until they gave up in disgust. Except for the *Santa Ana Register*, the system was news for only about a week. The *Register*, however, printed over twenty local news articles about the system before their editors felt it had been given sufficient coverage. From this source alone has come much of the advancement made by the system.

Following the A.P. news release came a flood of letters from all parts of the country. Most letters requested material and information, especially after a national newsletter for handicapped children proclaimed that it was free for the asking. Essentially that was correct but only on a very restricted and limited basis—free to prospective recruits whom I could teach. My mailing costs soared, my spare time disappeared, and yet no actual system advancement was in sight. Nevertheless, the newspaper publicity did accomplish three important things. It quickly broadcast word about the system to the general public. It brought some speaking engagements for me. And it built my second class of teachers for system instruction.

Fifteen people, mostly from the Orange County area, were taught in Fountain Valley one evening a week. The composition of the class was varied. I had elementary, junior high, and senior high teachers, as well as a middle aged couple who owned a private school. Since their interests were so varied I recognized the necessity for an adequate instruction booklet.

After I finished teaching that class, my son and I put together a fifty-page manual on system operations. It contained explanations and instructions to supplement my classroom instruction for starting the system. Over three months' time and large sums of money were spent on this project.

Also, as a result of that second class, the private school couple became so enthused that they requested my services for all twenty of their private school teachers. The only catch lay in their terms for doing so. In essence, I was to be paid for running their private school with the system. This was tempting indeed, since it would be an excellent demonstration of the system's prowess and could become the showcase I had long sought. But it could also become the system's grave if I couldn't get the right people to look at the results. The couple insisted on a long-term contract and a full-time devotion to their school. This would have knocked out my future expansion plans for the system. Very reluctantly I decided that the couple's price was too high, and since they wouldn't negotiate on their requirements, the opportunity was lost.

The newspaper publicity, together with the efforts of a friend, Barbara Taylor, did bring an opportunity to explain the system at Knott's Berry Farm. My audience was small but very select. The assistant superintendent of education for California was there with a number of school board members from various Orange County school districts. They all seemed impressed after my presentation and said that I would hear from them soon. And some were as good as their word.

The assistant superintendent, together with a professor from a local university, made a personal visit to several system classrooms in the Mono School District. Like all the administrators before them, they gave every indication of being impressed during the inspection but I never heard another word after their departure.

The only school board member from the Knott's Berry meeting to actively offer assistance was Robert Harr, formerly of the Santa Ana Unified School District. He worked diligently in the system's behalf, so much so that he found himself at odds with his school administrators and other board members. He was finally defeated at election time.

Mr. Harr is a dedicated freedom fighter who will stand up and be counted when wrongs need to be righted. But this was his downfall where politics are concerned. Instead of trying to pacify both sides and then the middle, Mr. Harr spoke his views on issue after issue. He honestly wanted to better education and he recognized and despised the "smoke without fire" machinations employed in this field.

First, Mr. Harr requested that his district administrators visit the system's classrooms in my district, which they did. Next, he succeeded in having his Santa Ana School Board approve a unit of inservice pay credit for any district instructor who would complete the system course. Finally, he tried hard to get his administrators and other board colleagues to accept an incentive bonus plan which would accomplish miracles in the field of education by allowing initiative to function inside the classroom. But he failed, as I warned him he would. Instead, another "smoke without fire" bonus program was voted into the Santa Ana School District, with all accountability in it carefully penciled out.

The bonus plan I devised for Mr. Harr's presentation to his Santa Ana School Board was, I felt, ingenious in that it reversed the customary education procedure—it actually saved money and cost nothing to implement. Maybe this was the reason for its quick defeat, but more than likely the accountability is what frightened its opponents. My plan hung education's wasteful practices out to dry. No longer would the "smoke without fire" philosophy be tolerated by a gullible public. Every taxpayer could readily see if funds were being misused and wasted. And, at last, honest effort inside the classroom would be rewarded by objective measurement rather than the inaccurate opinions of superiors who were frequently advocates of the "smoke without fire" philosophy.

My bonus plan functions in the following manner: The source of the funds to pay the bonus is derived from the salary which is saved when any teacher *voluntarily* requests a classroom load beyond thirty pupils (or other arbitrary class size as good teaching practices for the particular grade level or classroom demand). To compute the bonus a few simple calculations must be made:

a. The teacher's per pupil salary is determined by dividing his annual salary by thirty (the average classload of an average teacher).

<u>e.g.</u> $9,000   30 pupils $300 per pupil
         Annual Salary   ÷   (Hypothetical   =   Salary
         (Hypothetical)   and arbitrary)

b. The overall achievement average for each particular class is computed by dividing the total number of school years the whole class has been in school (allowing ten months for each school year) into the total years achieved academically by the students, as measured by a good standard achievement test given during the last weeks of each school year (instead of at the beginning as is done now).

c. The teacher's achievement bonus is based upon the increase measured over the classroom average for all previous school years. This bonus would also be multiplied by the number of extra pupils beyond thirty.

d. Thus, classroom size could and would grow (and save many tax dollars and the cost of the bonus) only if the students' academic achievement also increased. Either way a school district could never lose if any teacher voluntarily elected to try the bonus plan. Teachers who couldn't increase achievement averages with more than thirty pupils should expect a customary salary while those who could would receive an earned bonus for their efforts.

e. By testing at the end of the year, rather than at the beginning, many desirable results would become available, such as: (1) Educational accountability. (2) Results would be available to the teacher, rather than just to the next instructor who couldn't care less. (3) Pupils would be tested before summer vacation rather than after, when minds have laid dormant.

With such a bonus plan as this operating inside any school district I felt sure that the sick business of education could rapidly recover. I tried to point out this fact to its opponents in the Santa Ana School District by citing the age-old business adage that "more production with fewer people results in larger profits to spend." They wouldn't listen. I also tried to explain that my plan would require no change from present procedures. Teachers' salary schedules would be the same and the instructor with more longevity or a better education would still rise on the salary scale in the same way. But they weren't interested. Desperately I tried to assure everyone that nothing in the present educational scheme of things would be disturbed by implementing my incentive bonus plan except that children would get a better education through teacher motivation and accountability. But this was sufficient to give some administrators a scare and even worry the local teachers association officials. All could visualize their particular educational empire crumbling through the need for fewer teachers.

The Santa Ana administrators tried to employ me as a district consultant to teach the system to a core of about twenty hand-picked teachers. I refused their generous monetary offer for the reason that such an arrangement made the system subject to administrative manipulations and perversions which I would have been powerless to prevent. From the beginning, I had been tender about this point, so much so that I required a contract from each recruit which restricted system instruction. I wanted my system users to teach it to others but only with my supervision until they had sufficient experience of their own. Anything else, I felt, would adversely reflect on those already using it correctly. Therefore, when the Santa Ana administrators insisted upon unrestricted use of the system, I refused to teach it to their instructors. The rumor then spread that I was trying to control teaching methods, the teachers themselves, and even classroom philosophies. Naturally, this frightened any new recruit and reduced my Santa Ana efforts to zero.

As if this wasn't bad enough, the president of the Santa Ana teacher's association publicly proclaimed that he felt the system was an insidious attempt to indoctrinate little children in capitalistic philosophy which would make them "money grubbers." This statement was made without adequate knowledge of the system. I had long begged this association's administrators for the opportunity to present the system to their members. The association's executive director seemed interested but never managed to secure permission from his board of directors.

The association opposition caught me off guard since the system helped the individual classroom teacher as much as her pupils. Its autonomous power made her almost independent of outside pressures. But it was here that I could see the association's objections. Associations, like school districts, are built on power structures. What may be good for their individual members may not be, and usually isn't, good for the administrators' power. Again, more students per teacher reduces empires and any system that would reduce the individual teacher's dependence would probably never be viewed favorably by any administrator.

Perhaps the most frustrating weapon available to, and utilized by, my opposition was the refusal to investigate the system unless I presented concrete evidence of prior success. Especially frustrating was the fact that the means for obtaining such proof lay almost exclusively within the hands of the very people who demanded such proof. Finally I came to realize that the administrators didn't really want this proof. With it, they would have no good reason to refuse me. I held this opinion about every administrator until I met Dr. Daniel Fischer.

Dr. Fischer holds every educational credential offered by the State of California. He has been named "Orange County Educator of the Year" and was formerly one of the top administrators in the Santa Ana School District. Dr. Fischer is more than well qualified in the field of education. Not only does he possess two doctorates, but he also became a millionaire at thirty-seven through his own business acumen.

Dr. Fischer's mind is sharp and his disposition pragmatic. When he and I and the system were brought together by Dr. Peterson, he became one of the system's enthusiastic supporters. However, due to the very qualities I found so wonderful, Dr. Fischer was considered somewhat of a maverick in education. At the time I met him he was unemployed, with few districts seeking the services of such an outspoken critic.

It wasn't until August 1970 that I received a telephone request to teach the system to all of Dr. Fischer's instructors at his newly-acquired school district in Warner Springs, California. I accommodated him that fall with great pleasure. This could be the opportunity for which I had been looking, I thought then. What did it matter that his school district contained only eight teachers from kindergarten through eighth grade, and 150 kids? His district could become a showcase that would outweigh even the hundred teachers who were then using the system throughout Southern California. By employing the complete program under a capable and sympathetic school administrator, I could point the way for other tax-supported schools. But what I failed to realize is that a purposely-ignored showcase is just as useless as none at all. The previous school year should have taught me that lesson but it didn't. The previous year, my own school district had ignored all the startling facts regarding the supposedly unique showcase of fifty-five pupils described previously. At the start of that year my school board had listened to my official presentation of the system and the pilot program, then in progress, without comment or action. No one from the Mono administrative staff or school board had seemed interested enough even to visit my classroom. And when the school year closed, the administrators refused even to recognize the results of their own Stanford Achievement Tests in all subject areas. Though my classroom full of rejects and discipline problems *doubled their previous achievement average*, my administrators said they didn't see anything significant. Even after I broke my arm, toward the end of the school year, and two instructors took my place, no one admitted that the system had done anything unusual.

As I write this now and look back on the situation, it seems the height of stupidity to have expected anything different from Dr. Fischer's showcase except more frustration. But being human, I did.

After three months of system use in one school, the Warner Springs School District tested all pupils with the complete Stanford Achievement Battery. They discovered their achievement average had tripled, and Dr. Fischer was elated. He tried to give the measurements to his county superintendent of education. But, as Dr. Fischer relates, "Nobody seemed to be interested." He did receive a perfunctory visit from the county psychologist. When he told me about it, I said that the good head doctor had probably been sent more to examine Dr. Fischer than his kids or the system.

Such callous treatment aroused Dr. Fischer, and he blew the lid off the whole experiment by giving the facts to the *San Diego Union*. A fine article appeared but it only further strained relations between Dr. Fischer and his administrative colleagues. Finally, after suffering more rebuffs in his efforts to interest other educators, Dr. Fischer gave all of the shameful facts to a local weekly newspaper located at nearby Julian, California, which printed them as received. I never heard what the results were of this, but most probably nothing good for Dr. Fischer.

Some of Dr. Fischer's statements are quoted from this *Ramona Sentinel* article by Tom Griffin, dated March 25, 1971:

"Wouldn't you think that educators and the county schools office would be interested in any system of education that could produce such astonishing achievements, the superintendent asked. But they are not interested, he said. 'I asked him what he thought of our achievement test results at Warners,' he continued, 'and he said he would not comment upon it.'

"Educators are inclined to shun Dr. Fischer's programs, he believes, because he is teaching capitalism, and the educational trend is running strongly in the opposite direction. 'Leaders in education,' he says, 'say we are to prepare children for life. This is what we are doing in Warners,' he said."

* * *

"Our capitalistic system is based upon and remains vigorous because of competition, he believes.

" . . . [A]nd then they're not prepared for competition. They haven't been taught to compete, instead have been overprotected. Our public schools are incubators to keep students warm and secure. Then when the egg hatches after eight years of elementary school and four years of secondary education he is expected to be full grown and able to compete. And education is not preparing them for that in any way.

" 'Therefore,' he said, 'education today is not implementing its basic premise, that is, preparing children to live in our society. Instead educators are teaching along the lines of what they hope society will be.' College educators are training teachers to prepare children for a future society, not as society is today. They teach security in the schools, not independence and motivation."

* * *

" 'The system is upside down,' Fischer states. 'The basic problem with the schools is that students are taught the abstract and then go to the concrete after they graduate. What we should do is reverse our educational approach to resemble real life and start with the concrete and finish with the abstract. The abstract teachings will give the basis for finding solutions to problems of the concrete such as math, buying a home, buying a car, the stock market, to show how math is used in building a home, to determine costs involved. Does it pay to rent or pay to own? All these concepts could be taught from the concrete to the abstract.' "

* * *

"At our school we glorify academics instead of sports. We must return to the original concept that sports are entertainment and that academics is what schools are all about," Fischer said.

"According to Dr. Fischer, the Warner students are so competitively fired up with the Harrison System that the achievement night, recently held, held much more excitement than any sporting event. The atmosphere was electric in a packed auditorium where every student received an award (and justified) for his academic gains."

If even the most mighty of educators couldn't buck the administrative establishment, how could a teacher like me ever expect to do so? Fool that I am, I still chose to try.

I allowed myself to be scheduled for various speaking engagements. Some of the more prominent were as follows:

(1) To a number of local colleges and school districts.

(2) To the quarterly luncheon meeting of the Santa Ana Chamber of Commerce.

(3) To an audience of approximately 400 educators at Saddleback High School in Santa Ana.

(4) To various political groups locally.

(5) Finally, I presented the system to the annual gathering of the Christian Economics Foundation, as a guest speaker alongside such notables as Dr. Howard Kershner, Ed Rowe and Dr. Rushdooney, with an audience of a thousand.

Despite my best efforts, the spread of the system could be measured by the width of a flea's knee. The apathy of the public was unbelievable. This apathy, I came to realize, allows the "smoke without fire" philosophy to flourish so successfully. In fact, this is the only reason for its existence. People outside of education don't know how to appreciate educational progress and, on the contrary, frequently view it with suspicion. These were conclusions I had drawn from the past.

It was at this point that I almost gave up, but there remained one last mountain to climb. The private school field was a mysterious monster which everyone said I should have tried first. So I again started up the cliffs to even more frustrations.

CHAPTER 14
The Private School
Operating My Own School

With a nervous stomach made worse by so many frustrations, and after experiencing a broken arm which now ached continuously, my health broke down. I applied for and received a two-year sabbatical leave from my school district and I entered the hospital for an intestinal operation. About the time I emerged from the hospital, I met Professor Jones.

Professor Jones had been exposed to some of the system's publicity, and, as a business consultant he visualized commercial possibilities for it. He and I tried to form an enterprise to explore all angles. However, due to basic differences in opinions, we amicably dissolved our association, but before we did a number of advances had been made in the system.

A contract with Azusa Pacific College was negotiated whereby graduate-level credit could be given to system recruits for twenty-one-, thirty-six-, and fifty-four-hour courses taught under the high-quality educational standards of that school. I was beside myself with pleasure and pride. For the first time, higher level education had recognized the value of the system. Perhaps other educators might now be induced to take a look. But my hope was still forlorn. Despite many mailed brochures explaining what was offered, I received few replies.

Next, Professor Jones tried to interest some of his former business associates and friends in the franchising of private schools using the system. He met nothing but frustrations in this endeavor and eventually he also was hospitalized for an abdominal operation.

Finally, I came up with the idea of renting unoccupied Sunday school facilities for our proposed chain of private schools. This seemed like the perfect solution to a very difficult problem. Previously, we had hit a brick wall from the cost angle for facilities. The various bureaucracies, such as the building department, the fire department, and the health department all demanded expensive installations wherever children were taught. Therefore, if we could obtain facilities already equipped for instruction, I reasoned, our expenses could be cut and the church's revenue increased.

Professor Jones and I mailed hundreds of letters to all Orange County churches requesting an interview to discuss our mutual needs. We received about seven or eight replies and ended up with one actual church board approval for a private school. This was granted by the Church of the Brethren at 502 South Ross Street, in Santa Ana. My spirits soared, but again the future would quickly dampen that. It seemed as if my frustrations would never cease. After Professor Jones wisely decided to drop out, I picked up his frustrations as well as my own.

Very fortunately for me, my progress became joined with a man who changed my life more than any other human outside of my family. Pastor Forest Groff of the Church of the Brethren assisted me every way he could in the establishment of the Harrison Free Enterprise Elementary School as well as spiritually to a better life.

The first obstacle we encountered became the Santa Ana Planning Commission. This august body turned down our request for a conditional use permit to operate a private school in a Sunday school facility. We discovered that a neighborhood petition had been raised against the school by a local resident who was extremely unhappy with the church's location next to her rental property. We appealed to the Santa Ana City Council and won with a larger counter-petition of neighborhood signatures, but not without a further struggle with the fire department. Since the local code demanded it, our Sunday school building, used as a private school, had to have an expensive fire alarm and sprinkler system. Also we were required to modify the building since we would be utilizing it more than the church congregation. The wonderful church members donated their time and I paid for the materials. The alterations were finished just in time for the summer school to start.

The enrollment for the private school was built with such exhaustive effort and large expense that I hate to write about it even now. I couldn't afford to wait for pupils to enroll, as some better schools do.

I had no reputation to influence parents. In fact I had none of the normal goodies associated with private education. I had a church Sunday school building with religious posters on the wall which, for some unexplained reason, seemed to make my prospective parents think that their child would be indoctrinated in a religion rather than scholarship. There were no beautiful grounds to attract the eye and the City Council had restricted all of the school playground and physical education activities to the inside of the Sunday school building because of the complaining neighbors. Also I had not yet purchased any education materials since I couldn't be certain of having any pupils. Not having had any income for over a year, I was in no position to spend money on possible economic bubbles. Even now it's almost impossible for me to imagine how I convinced fifteen different parents to enroll their children in my penurious school for the summer rather than any of the other impressive institutions available throughout Orange County.

I spent large sums I could ill afford from my family's grocery money, for attractive school brochures. Then I rented a telephone answering service. After all, I needed some semblance of a business front to convince parents that I wouldn't take their money and run. In the absence of any reputation for scholarship, I knew that some type of advertising would be necessary. I counted heavily upon the articles about the system that had been run in the *Santa Ana Register* to bring in some business, which they did. And that fine newspaper even printed a few more about the school itself, which helped. My whole family called door to door as we passed out brochures throughout the Orange County area. An advertisement in the weekly "Pennysaver," a classified sheet mailed to local homes, also helped. But probably of most value was the advertising assistance given by the *Santa Ana Register* and its kind publisher, Mr. Hoiles. Actually, I felt fortunate indeed. Probably no private school anywhere started with a better chance for survival from advertising coverage.

For three months I drove the forty-five miles daily between Riverside and Santa Ana trying to gather pupils for summer school. I called on 120 parents in their homes, using a flip chart to explain the system, before enrolling fifteen pupils during the last week. I was discouraged at such a slim showing until I talked with a few other private-school owners. Fifteen was quite normal for a first summer school, it seemed, especially when my program was almost exclusively academic outside of the auctioned trips. Many parents, they said, feel as I always have:

when a child studies hard during the regular school year he deserves a rest for the summer.

From the beginning I had determined that my private school would be different from the conventional, and even different from the three or four then using my system. I planned on a number of drastic changes, so drastic that a number of my colleagues and friends thought I was either a fool or crazy for implementing them.

"You can't pay your teachers in accordance with the number of pupils they instruct," I was told time and again. "No teacher will work for you."

Yet, that is exactly what I did. My teachers received half of each pupil's $50 monthly tuition. With a guaranteed minimum of ten students, the instructor was paid $250 monthly and $25 for each additional pupil beyond.

Fortunately for me, I opened the summer school with three family members as instructors—my wife, my son, and myself. With an enrollment of only fifteen pupils (three of these withdrew later), I could pay my son only a token salary of $100 for his six weeks of teaching and my wife and I drew no money at all. Most of the school's meager income went for educational supplies, rent to the church, and a phone.

I had determined that the pupils in my private school would be unchained from the usual lock-step type of education where all students march through textbooks together. Instead of all working in the same textbook and at the same level, each child could progress at his or her own rate from one workbook to another. Thus individual achievement would be accomplished.

To achieve this worthy goal, I bought ditto masters for all grade levels and for all normally-taught subjects. I paid over $200 for ditto paper and invested $375 in a new duplicating machine. Then I ran off hundreds of booklets which my family put together on donated time. For two months we worked night and day on the project. Whenever a child finished a workbooklet, which usually took the place of a textbook, his parents would pay forty cents (my cost) for another. It was a real joy to watch the system motivate pupils into working through one booklet after another. And with system techniques available, individualized instruction did not become the problem it does in the conventional classroom.

However, a few unexpected problems did arise. The first was the attitude of the pupils. They felt that a summer school should be strictly fun, with subjects geared to this philosophy, such as swimming, arts, and crafts. When my students discovered that the school was almost exclusively academic, without even a physical education program, they became restless and weren't as satisfied as I expected them to be within the system. Also, I couldn't begin to operate the system properly with such a small number of pupils in each of our three classrooms. The system is designed to function best with a large class where pupils help each other and run the classroom with adult guidance. My son, my wife, and eventually I, all had to retreat to conventional methods which defeated the purpose of the system and the school. To state the fact boldly, my private school had degenerated into a common run-of-the-mill school.

On top of everything, my broken arm now hurt like a toothache: the pain was intensified with the normal classroom tension, and parental problems which arise in any school where tuition is paid. After six weeks of this torture, I felt I had taken enough. The only solution was for me to get out of the classroom and become the school director exclusively. This I would do in the fall for the regular school year.

As September approached I became more and more depressed with the lack of enrollments. In spite of large sums (at least they were large for me) spent to acquire pupils, I had only eight pupils signed up. Again, my family passed out brochures from door to door and I called personally at the homes of prospective parents to explain the merits of the system. I covered Orange County day and night and even solicited pupils as far away as Los Angeles County. I realized that I might be biting off more than I could chew when it came time to transport pupils. But I was desperate for enrollments. I needed at least thirty pupils, ten for each of my three proposed classrooms. Anything less than three rooms would make too large a grade spread for one teacher to handle most efficiently. I planned to have a primary room—kindergarten through first grade; an intermediate room—second grade through fourth grade; and an advanced room—fifth grade through eighth grade.

The transportation of pupils could be solved by the parents hauling the children, I decided. Those mothers who were willing to transport additional children for a monthly sum of about fifteen or twenty dollars would be put in touch with other parents from the same locality. All arrangements and operations were left in the hands of the respective parents. As the school progressed, everything seemed to be satisfactory for those concerned, at least regarding transportation.

We opened our school doors the middle of September 1971 with a final paid enrollment of thirty-four pupils. My family members became the three classroom instructors, with the school directorship reserved for me. Our library and textbook supply had been built from the castoffs scrounged from the local tax-supported schools. These books were out-of-date and considered unusable. I was most grateful to get them as there were no surplus funds for such purchases in my private school.

The first problem to rear its ugly head was, again, pupil attitudes. In my desperate search for enrollments, I did not screen students. I accepted one and all gratefully. Much to my consternation, and my older son's misery, we found his advanced-level classroom loaded with the worst kind of discipline problems—pupils who had been refused admission almost everywhere else.

Inasmuch as this was my son's first year of full time teaching after his college graduation and a year of public school substituting, I decided that I would eliminate six of his worst discipline problems. Even so, more than half of his remaining sixteen students were "wall climbers" of the worst sort. The school was then down to a total enrollment of twenty-eight. This, I guessed at the time, would probably decline further before it ever began to rebuild. I knew that it usually took a while for dissatisfactions to set in at other private or tax-supported schools.

So the big question arose: Should I quit then or was the prospect bright enough to continue? Many factors had to be considered. Foremost was the welfare of the pupils. They should not be hurt in the process. And how about the church and its hopeful expectations for revenue after helping to modify its Sunday school facilities? And what would all the system-enthused parents think and feel about any disbanding at this early stage without what they might consider a fair trial?

On the other side of the slate lay the personal considerations regarding myself and my family. Could I ask my family to teach for beggar's wages? Was I willing to continue for perhaps the whole school year without any salary and probably pour even more of my own money into a losing operation? Also, and probably the most important question, was I willing to abandon most of the system and teach conventionally with small classes?

My family and I decided to continue, but with a drastic change for me. I was to return to classroom teaching. My older son would become the school director and I would take his classroom long enough to tame the lions and tigers still to be found there. When this task had been accomplished, we could hopefully hire a teacher to take this class. Thus I would eventually be free to try and build enrollment.

I lasted about six weeks before the ache in my arm drove me out. The daily tension became unbearable and I found myself taking it out on my family and pupils. It became a great test of willpower to hold my feelings inside. I ran an advertisement in the *Santa Ana Register* for a teacher willing to teach for $250 monthly. Much to my surprise, I had twenty-five applicants begging for the opportunity. But the actual selection was limited to just a few. Most prospects were so socialistically oriented that I would have been frightened to let them anywhere near my students. And the rest demanded respectable compensation for their teaching time, which I was in no position to offer.

Finally I narrowed my choice to an experienced classroom instructor who possessed a doctorate in divinity, and a nonexperienced woman with a B.A. degree. Both seemed enthused with the system. I decided to hire them both since both of my teaching sons now wanted to dissolve their association with the school. They had visions of travel and the good life with a decent salaried position elsewhere. I couldn't find it in my heart to blame them. After all, each had worked like a slave for a mere pittance of $250 monthly and they looked at my own unsalaried example for future prospects.

I held a class in Harrison System methods twice a week for two and a half weeks, and then I brought my two new teachers into their prospective classrooms. Gradually these raw recruits assumed complete control. Such a short training period for such a vast system was, I knew, completely inadequate and unrealistic. This was readily apparent to any classroom observer but, I felt, there was little else I could do. No system teacher was available anywhere who would be willing to teach at my school for the pittance I could pay. And I knew my health wouldn't permit further training time to say nothing about the expense. Fortunately, my two new instructors had agreed to train and teach for the first month at half pay. This allowed me to keep my financial head above the surface. Paying both the new teachers and my sons would have strained our finances beyond the breaking point.

Meanwhile, during this period, the enrollment dropped lower and lower until it reached twenty-four pupils, and some of these were not paying on time. I was desperate. Twenty-four students were insufficient to support three classroom teachers. I reduced to just two classrooms by consolidating pupils. This, I knew at the time, would breed many problems, but I felt my hands were financially tied to such a course of action. I couldn't ask any teacher to work for less than $200 monthly and my expenses didn't seem to reduce along with the enrollment.

Immediately my problems began to multiply. My new teacher with the doctorate had been a church pastor too long and an upper grade instructor whose adaptation to primary children was difficult to say the least. He disliked taking the academic dollars for infractions of the rules, and struggled daily to operate the system properly. Slowly he seemed to improve, and under the circumstance, I felt he was doing an admirable job. My other new teacher seemed to adapt to the system quite well. However, her lack of classroom experience, her lack of subject knowledge, and the ability to dispense it to pupils, were handicaps.

Earlier in the school year my family had helped me to mail letters to all the churches in the Seattle, San Francisco and San Jose areas, inquiring about the use of their Sunday school facilities. Our interest in this had been generated by a voucher plan the federal government proposed to install in these areas. Here was an opportunity I had long sought for the system. Enrollment-building would be easy when no money would need to be pried from prospective parents. We received sixteen interested replies from churches in the solicited areas and then the government abandoned its plan. I had to write a letter of retraction to each because of this and also included my declining health as an additional reason.

It wasn't until about December that I really saw the handwriting on the wall. My arm then ached so badly that I hated to set foot inside the classroom and I began, once again, to take my frustrations and pain out on my family and the pupils. I realized that it was over for me and I had to quit then or else I would break down completely. With no medical insurance, my financial plight would be serious. The only question to be answered was: How could I get out and hurt the fewest people?

I decided to make a clean breast of it all to the good pastor of the Church of the Brethren. I explained that my arm hurt and I felt that the warm sunshine of Florida or the Virgin Islands might help. Also that I had an opportunity to start a school in Florida as I had done in California, if my health ever improved.

Pastor Groff listened with sympathy but disagreed when I suggested that the school be closed. He felt that the new instructors were capable of carrying on with the system and the school. I was naturally hesitant since the reputation of the Harrison System was at stake if my inadequately-trained teachers couldn't carry the ball. My wife strongly suggested that I should close the school.

Finally I agreed to leave the school open and installed a parental school board for policy control. Next, I made the instructor with a doctorate my school director and gave him complete charge of the school. At one time previous to this I had entertained thoughts of selling the school until I realized that this might degrade the system if I should acquire the wrong buyer.

Back in July or August my family and I had forseen the need for a nonprofit foundation to operate the chain of schools we had planned. I spent over $500 acquiring a corporation charter from the State of California which we used to operate our Santa Ana private school. When we decided to turn the school's operation over to the newly hired teachers and its parental school board, I also appointed a managing director for the affairs of the foundation.

Mr. Charles Billings, a high school teacher now using the system, took charge of the foundation and made himself available as a troubleshooter for our private school. Thus, it seemed to me, I had effectively covered every angle and nothing prevented my departure. After all, if this school couldn't stand on its own two feet and operate without my guiding hand on it constantly, there was no hope of establishing any more. And so I bowed out of the private school business for all practical purposes.

CHAPTER 15
The End

As my wife, my youngest son, and I headed toward Florida with our cabover camper pickup truck, I felt like a brand new man. Sure, I still had my sore arm and I was out of a job until next fall, but the terrible frustrations seemed to be left behind. What did it matter that I would be considered a failure by most standards? At least I was now free of complaining parents, unruly children, and the steadily mounting crisis which tore my stomach apart and magnified the pain in my arm.

Upon arrival in Key Largo, Florida, I began to rewrite this book for the fourth and last time. The words came slowly and I had to use my right arm sparingly for one-finger typing. It ached more and more each night, but the manuscript did progress. The warm Florida sun helped me keep going.

May 1972 arrived and I still had heard no word from my employer, the Mono Unified School District. I knew that teaching contracts were normally signed and sent out in March or April. Perhaps mine had been overlooked in the rush to dispense them. After all, there was probably no other teacher in the school district returning from a two year leave of absence. So I sent a request to both the district superintendent and my school board.

As the days passed without reply, I became alarmed. Evidently my administrators were really angry with me and intended to refuse me a teaching contract. Perhaps they had a right to be since they probably felt that I had cost the district far more than I was worth in both mental anxiety and actual cash.

Two years before this, and a month after I broke my arm, the acting superintendent of the Mono School District informed me that the pilot project concerning my fifty-five pupil classroom was no pilot project at all—it had never been officially approved by the school board. This meant that all the sixth grade teachers involved in this measurement program for the system had been working their hearts out for nothing. That information came out when the district administrators thought that they might have to classify my broken arm as an industrial accident (I broke it on one of the scheduled system trips with my pupils).

This seemed grossly unjust to me, especially since the pilot project and the system had been given wide dissemination. It had appeared in print, and my board members had listened to an explanation at their homes and in the Board Room. Some board members had allowed their sons or daughters to take the earned trips in my classroom and even in other classrooms of system teachers. Almost all the district administrators and officials were well aware of the working details concerning the system.

The district administrators allowed all the sixth grade teachers to continue with the "pilot project," special-testing their classes at the start and at the end of the school year, until my broken arm suddenly made it no pilot project. At the root of the reversal was the increased insurance rate it might cost the district. So I took my case to court at the suggestion of the acting superintendent.

The hearing was held in San Bernardino over two years later and a very fair-minded judge found that the accident was work-connected. I was declared to be forty-six and a quarter percent permanently disabled. Immediately the state lawyers for workmen's compensation set out to appeal this decision. This is where my case stands as of this writing. The State Compensation Fund has the privilege of continuously appealing the case until it reaches the Supreme Court whenever they don't like any lower court's decision. It could be years before any money changes hands. Meanwhile the unfortunate victim whistles for medical or financial assistance.

Evidently it was this unfavorable court decision which prompted my administrators to ignore my pleas for a teaching contract. They possibly felt that I would give up and go some place else for employment. But what they failed to realize is that I had no place else to go. They themselves have effectively seen to that by alerting other districts to the supposed evils inherent in me and the system. Further, my injured arm prevented much employment in other areas.

Finally I dispatched a registered letter, with a return receipt requested, to the district. I meant to have my old job back as a tenured teacher. It was either that or starvation, I felt. I didn't know whether I would be able to teach with my painful arm or not, but I surely wanted the chance to try.

The district received my request but still no reply came. Being ignorant of teacher tenure laws, I supposed that the district must have a signed contract from me on file not later than the thirtieth of June. When this date passed and still no contract, I headed for home.

In the middle of August I phoned the Mono District's director of personnel who informed me that my school board had still made no decision on my re-employment. I showed up physically for employment on the first of September and was informed that the school board was of the opinion that my re-employment would be refused based upon the court's forty-six and a quarter percent disability rating. I immediately mailed another request for employment to my school board.

Finally a telegram arrived from the director of personnel. I was to report for instructional duties the day after school started. Evidently someone in authority got smart at the last minute. My forced idleness could have cost the district plenty and they still wouldn't have been rid of me. So once more I am teaching in a tax-supported classroom. The cycle is now complete. However, also once again, the handwriting is on the wall. Every day of teaching seems to make the ache in my arm get a little worse. But this time I can't run off to the sunny climate of Florida. I'll have to stay and face the music. But of one thing I am sure, I will not stay if it means even a remote possibility of taking my pain and frustrations out on my pupils, especially when I know that my own school district doesn't want me or my system.

Just to make the dismal picture complete, I was recently informed that the charter for our nonprofit foundation has been suspended by the state for failure to file, of all things, an income tax form. As if that wasn't sufficient, the Church of the Brethren installed new nonsystem teachers in their Sunday school facilities for this school year. Further, I have learned that my school district has been busily about its usual business of harassing system teachers. During my absence, one instructor has been forced to resign after suffering a heart attack and another had to move to another school to escape the tender mercy of the principal. However one tiny ray of sunshine did peek through the gloom: it was recently announced that the director of personnel for the Mono School District would take employment with another school district. Perhaps this might begin new policy trends and administrative thinking for the future of my district, especially since my new school superintendent (appointed during my two year absence) probably doesn't hold any personal animosity toward me for my past mistakes.

CHAPTER 16
What the System Can Do for You

When I wrote my first book on the system, many years ago, I mentioned this fact to my sixth grade class. Immediately they wanted to know its title. I said, "Motivating Johnny." This brought forth blank stares until I tried to explain the word "motivation." One of my more precocious pupils volunteered his own definition.

"Oh! I know what *motorvating* means," Raymond said, with all the smugness a pupil can muster when only he knows the answer. "That's like when my pa has an old motor in his car that won't run. He just yanks it out and puts in another motor that will."

After a few moments thought I was forced to agree with Raymond. Perhaps I *was* writing about *Motorvating Johnny*. When the pupil's academic motor wouldn't run toward achievement the system replaced it with one that would.

The importance of motivation, I feel, can't be overemphasized. Little occurs inside the classroom, or outside of it, without motivation playing a part. Most experts in education have recognized the need to motivate Johnny but little has been done about it, because few educators know what to do. This is not just my opinion. It is the observation, for example, of Jack R. Frymier and James H. Thompson, in their article called "Motivation—the Learner's Mainspring," in the May 1965 issue of the *Educational Leader*. Frymier and Thompson indicate that much is known in the area of motivation but very little about what motivates pupils to try hard in school. The reason for this, they say, is lack of classroom research. They boldly state that educators know too little about what motivates students. They believe that, "theoretically, achievement in school is a function of past experiences and present experiencing."

So we discover that it is in the area of experiencing where most *conventional* teachers have their difficulties. This is sad and unnecessary since the Harrison System allows pupils to experience most phases of life in a way that most traditional methods can't match. System students discover that they want to learn for many reasons rather than just because of the age-old motivators advanced by the traditionalist educator, "love of learning" and a strong-willed teacher.

Personally, I have great admiration for the conventional classroom teacher. How he can continue to motivate his class with nothing other than his personality and ingenuity remains nothing short of a miracle. Yet some educators advocate the use of nothing else. As an example, Edwin John Brown and Arthur Thomas Phelps, in the book *Managing the Classroom—The Teacher's Part in School Administration*, state on page 164 that there should be no outside rewards because: "First, you are a poor teacher if you can't make the desired activity reasonably interesting to your pupils without using any artificial stimulation. And second, a child needs to have a wholesome respect for his duty and for his work, and there is no better self-discipline than holding himself to a task, though it be unpleasant."[1]

Realizing that such general motivational advice to a budding instructor is useless once the teacher actually enters the classroom (especially in a ghetto school), the teacher's colleges have attempted to be more practical and offer detailed instructions. So detailed that I had difficulty remembering them after reading through twice. I wondered how they could have any possible value for the novice instructor six months after they were read. The following is quoted from pages seventy-six and seventy-seven in a *Guide To Student Teaching*, by Leslie Nelson and Blanche McDonald, published by the William C. Brown Company of Dubuque, Iowa, in 1958:

> 4. The student teacher, who wishes to put "pep" into his teaching, does the following: a. Premeditates what the child is going to think or say. b. Motivates every lesson, starting with something that is part of the child's daily life. c. "Activates" every problem (dramatizes it). The problem of how to prevent the cloakroom from getting too crowded is quickly solved if it is actually dramatized. The student teacher telling

[1] Edwin John Brown and Arthur Thomas Phelps, *Managing the Classroom—The Teacher's Part in School Administration,* Second Edition, Copyright © 1961 The Ronald Press Company, New York.

how to prevent it is not enough. d. Introduces each lesson with: (1) An intriguing statement or (2) An interesting statement or (3) A challenging statement.

5. In studying about early cultures or peoples (Egyptians, Vikings, Pioneers, etc.) the student teacher should start with the present and go back to the past. He should never start with the past and lead up to the present. By so doing, he loses the interest of the class. For example; If the group is studying pioneers, he might start with life in a modern automobile trailer and then contrast it with life in a covered wagon.

6. Where books are used for reading, arithmetic, social studies, and language, the student teacher should have a "connecting line" in his motivation, such as "Now, let us open our books to see how Andy learned to be a lifeguard." He should never say, after a motivation, such a statement as this: "Open your books to page 34." If he does, the lesson "falls flat" and the motivation has been wasted.

I am afraid that, if I were to teach conventionally now, most of my lessons would fall flat. Can you imagine any teacher trying to implement these instructions all day long and day after day throughout the school year? Perhaps you can realize the vast amount of outside effort any teacher would need to expend for a successful day. And suppose it fell flat anyway, which it frequently does?

The system gives even the poorest instructor student incentives beyond belief every school day. I simply say, "Open your books to page thirty-four. Every problem on this page which you can work correctly is worth one dollar. If you need help, please hold up your hand and your student teacher will help you with it." Visitors to my room claim they can see smoke coming from every busy pencil.

Some education professors approach the motivation dilemma by being honest and admitting that they don't know what to advise. Two such worthy men are G. Max Wingo and Raleigh Schorling, who have written a book called *Elementary School Student Teaching*, published by McGraw-Hill Book Company of New York, Toronto, & London in 1955. This is what they say on page 212:

> You must understand that we can't tell you how to motivate Freddie Jones to learn to do two-column addition on February 21st. Neither can anyone else who does not know a great deal about Freddie, his ability in arithmetic, his previous knowledge, his attitude toward school, and the subject itself, together with a dozen other items. In other words, we will not give you devices and recipes.

Instead the teacher should try to present the material in such a way that Freddie needs to know it. Failing this, you may find you can't teach him by any method.

I'm sure that most ghetto teachers have found the previous sentence to be all too true. But the point I'm trying to make is that it doesn't need to be. Please observe some of the Stanford Achievement Test results I can quote after utilizing the Harrison System:

(1) In the pilot project cited earlier, with a sixth grade averaging fifty-five pupils in a self-contained classroom possessing an average IQ of 94, the average achievement gain is as follows for a *six month period*.

Word Meaning	Paragraph Meaning	Total Reading	Spelling	Language	Arithmetic Computation	Arithmetic Concepts	Arithmetic Application	Social Science	Science	Class Average
1.3	.6	1.0	1.2	1.1	1.4	.4	1.5	1.1	.9	1.06

The above figures indicate the school *years* gained academically by the average pupil in this classroom for the six months actually spent in the effort. For instance, the total reading advance for the average child was one year in six months, and the class average for all subjects was one year and six tenths of a month (1.06) in an actual six-month period, or about double the national average, which is one year of academic gain for each year's effort.

If the above achievement gain doesn't seem fantastic, perhaps the reader may appreciate it more if he realizes that the expected gain (that experienced in the past), with this same group of pupils for a six month period, was four and a half months. And this class, remember, was composed of the rejects from other teachers in the district.

To substantiate the system as the cause, I can quote even more fantastic gains in Jim Pecan's class of twenty-eight pupils in the same pilot project. For instance his pupils averaged a three-year gain in arithmetic computation in the same six-month period.

To further reveal the extent of the system's motivation prowess I would like to set forth Dr. Fischer's whole school district gain by grade levels in a *three month* period:

1st	.73 to 1.6	= 9 mo. gain
2nd	1.7 to 2.4	= 7 mo. gain
3rd	2.7 to 3.5	= 8 mo. gain
4th	3.4 to 4.5	= 1 yr., 1 mo. gain
5th	3.6 to 4.6	= 1 yr. gain
6th	4.8 to 5.9	= 1 yr., 1 mo.
7th	5.6 to 6.5	= 9 mo. gain
8th	6.7 to 7.5	= 8 mo. gain

The system tripled the achievement average for Dr. Fischer, but of even more importance are the byproducts he obtained at the same time. These necessary ingredients to a good education, I feel, are missing in the conventional classroom and their loss is rapidly destroying the society we have known and loved in the past.

Other educators have also noted this defect in conventional classrooms. To illustrate, I will quote from a November 1966 article, *"New Approaches to Educational Outcomes,"* in *Educational Leadership*, written by Earl C. Kelly:

"The good citizen who participates in the affairs of his community and of the world, who cares for his neighbors, must be considered to have had a good education. Whether he remembers what the Missouri Compromise was, for example, is not harmful, but irrelevant."

Later in the same article Professor Kelly also states "Whatever we do, it should result in our young becoming more loving, less hostile, more courageous, less fearful, more free, less enslaved.

"This form of assessment will bring about better, more adequate human beings. This, as I see it, is the task of the school, and the hope of humanity."

Hooray for Professor Kelly! You would think everyone would heed his advice in each classroom, but this doesn't appear to be the case. I don't believe that I need to recite the many social ills facing society today which have resulted either directly or indirectly from unmotivated and miseducated youth. The list runs from crime to welfare and from drugs to unpatriotic behavior. Search where you will, few social maladies can be found that are not, I feel, attributable to the classroom training youngsters now receive with conventional teaching methods. Perhaps this statement seems overly strong but it certainly bears investigation to try and prove it wrong. The situation in this country is certainly that serious.

For instance, the average child today goes from kindergarten through college without really knowing and understanding his fellow students, let alone his fellow man. He is so busy pursuing his own affairs that the difficulties of anyone else are completely ignored. Each child is encouraged to tend to his own business. Only in physical education is the rule really relaxed.

This lack of simple friendship and concern bears fruit in many ugly ways. Bystanders calmly watch as crimes are committed next to them. The good samaritan runs over the man bleeding in the street rather than become involved. The upstanding average citizen joins the mob and beats off the police in the normal discharge of their duties while upholding the law. Ghettos have now become a "no man's land" where even the police fear to enter.

And where can the blame be specifically laid? Most law enforcement officers would probably sum it all up in one word: "permissiveness!" I feel that a little more descriptive phrase would be "lack of responsibility." The children coming from our schools today exhibit very little sense of responsibility, I feel, because of the fact that none has been demanded of them inside the classroom.

If the Harrison System brings nothing to the classroom other than pupil responsibility, it is well worth implementation. When a student learns that he and he alone is responsible for his actions, all society benefits. If Johnny realizes that fighting on the playground will bring a heavy "academic dollar" fine, he will later believe that shooting his neighbor or spitting in the face of the police will also merit punishment. This realization must be instilled early to avoid the opposite from cementing itself.

The system provides training early, when it counts most. As a society, we are terrible when it comes to "an ounce of prevention." We will spend billions on cures and pennies on prevention. This is particulaly true when it comes to education. William F. Johntz, in his January 1967 *California Teacher's Association Journal* article, "Innovation and New Concern for the Disadvantaged," states:

> The new concern for the disadvantaged students in our schools is resulting in still another automatic benefit to education in general. This benefit results from the fact that when educators work seriously with the disadvantaged student, they inevitably rediscover the monumental importance of the tritest of all educational cliches, "an ounce of prevention is worth a pound of cure." They are discovering that $100 of their pre-

cious compensatory education funds spent at the elementary level is effecting more salutary change than $1,200 spent at the secondary level. Our present allocation of the public school dollar among the various grade levels is the single greatest irrationality in our entire educational system.

Someday, somewhere, a superintendent of exceptional courage and imagination will stop simply talking about the importance of preventing education problems at the elementary level rather than patching them up at the secondary level. He will go before his school board to request a major reallocation of district funds, not only federal funds, from the secondary level to the elementary level. Secondary education will be temporarily disallocated, but the ultimate result will be a vastly improved secondary school system when students enter the seventh grade truly prepared for a secondary education.

I would suggest then that the single most important innovation that will come out of our new concern with the disadvantaged will be to place elementary school education in its proper position in the educational grade level spectrum.

It's human nature to give the squeaking wheel the grease, and spend most of our meager educational funds on older mischief makers. Instead, let's follow Dr. Johntz's advice and implement the Harrison System in the elementary school and eliminate the need for costly cures later. The pupil who has experienced the system from kindergarten through junior high school probably won't need it afterward. Just because a kindergartener doesn't exhibit a propensity toward slugging his teacher with a blackjack this doesn't mean that these tender years of training can be blithely ignored. "For so the twig is bent, so the tree is inclined."

If I were to put my finger on the single most valuable contribution of the Harrison System to society it would have to be the system's ability to inculcate a sturdy individualism in pupils rather than the collectivism now forced upon youngsters in the conventional classroom. Unimaginable future harm is being generated with the dictatorial and socialistic methods practiced in most elementary schools. I believe that it isn't that schools can avoid failures (for even Russia has more than its share of these) but rather that all failures should have the *opportunity* to succeed through their own efforts and learn to profit from their mistakes.

Perhaps I'm mistaken, but I have always supposed that the purpose of schools is to prepare students for a life after graduation. If this is so, present conventional teaching methods should delight collectivists and horrify most Americans. I feel that a good many of our social problems today are rooted in this educational defect.

Family life is attacked constantly, but nothing acceptable to the average American is offered as a substitute. Religion is degraded in favor of devil worship. Unpatriotic behavior is advanced as the socially acceptable thing to do. Blacks are told that whitey hates them and vice versa. The utopian approach to most social problems is proposed in many colleges without question. Johnny is advised that the world owes him a living. It's easy today to get people to follow the leader, no matter how illogical he may be. They were conditioned as youngsters to a life of passivity and utopian dreams.

Children in elementary through junior high school are seldom allowed to think for themselves and pay the prescribed penalty if they make a mistake. Why in the world we still expect them to do so as an adult is beyond me. Yet we religiously do and are extremely disappointed when even the brightest can seldom do more than parrot his teacher. It's only after we have been severely burned several times as an adult that life's lessons are absorbed. Again, perhaps I'm wrong, but this seems to add up to a wasted education. Nowhere does this seem more evident than in the ghetto and barrio.

Few teachers, let alone middle-class citizens, realize the horrible task that confronts the educator in the slum areas of America. The typical middle class American pictures poor "Slum Johnny" as a child of the streets who has to struggle hard to get an education, with his barren homelife preventing any financial or academic assistance from the family. And his middle-class oriented teacher is portrayed as helping him in this mighty struggle to achieve something—anything. The subject matter he likes best, and of which he absorbs the most, is culture related to his ethnic descent. But his low IQ and disadvantaged background finally prevails and prevents him from acquiring the fine education he ardently desires.

Hogwash! Most educators in a position to know claim that the disadvantaged child hates school and stays there only until he can find work or drop out. If this is a fact, then it is a terrible indictment of education which borders on the criminal since it can so easily be remedied by applying principles basic to human nature.

What child, coming from such undesirable surroundings and background, could resist school if it were a place of fun and achievement? How could such a disadvantaged youngster fail to acquire an excellent education when learning was truly enjoyable? But facts *do* substantiate that school is viewed as a place of torture and nowhere is this more evident than in the ghetto.

Many educators, investigating school conditions in slum areas, have come away with the true picture of pupil attitudes. One such is Martin Deutsch who reveals his reaction in a *Society for Applied Anthropology* article of 1960 called "Minority Group and Class Status as Related to Social and Personality Factors in Scholastic Achievement," at Lafferty Hall, University of Kentucky: "This inconsistency between the lack of internalized reward anticipations on the part of the Negro child and his teacher's expectations that he does have such anticipations reflects the disharmony between the social environment of the home and the middle-class oriented demands of the school."

A few of the more perspicacious educational investigators have recognized that more of the same old classroom bandaids will not get the big job accomplished. Notice what Robert Strom has to say in his book, *Teaching in the Slum School*, published by Charles E. Merrill & Company of Columbus, Ohio, in 1965:

> Most of us agree that for a teacher to deny a child understanding and affection is to deny him an education. Without these elements of response, the slum child will reject school as he rejects life outside the institution. Nonetheless, some of us persist in maintaining higher priority for concerns of how teaching proceeds than of how learning occurs. As a consequence, the perfection of individualized instruction has been perceived as simply a matter of lower pupil-teacher ratio, better systems of grouping, and more time per child. Certainly something more than increased time and organization is needed to effectively instruct those who appear disinterested, their fellows who are belligerent, others who are slow and the remaining host of differing personalities in each classroom. What is required is a greater knowledge of learners and the learning process, more appropriate diagnostic measures to determine scholastic weakness, and methods of teaching that are in conjunction with each pupil's most efficient learning style and pace of accommodation. In short, what is called for is the highest form of respect: understanding.

The real problem in education everywhere is not a lack of perspicacious educators, for almost everyone recognizes that present methods aren't doing the job, but rather a lack of innovative teachers who can and will actually do something constructive about it. The Harrison System, I feel, is the perfect tool for remedying many defects found in slum-area classrooms. Not only will the turned-off pupil become enthusiastic but he will also receive training in a miniature life-like society which will condition him not only to want to compete with his more fortunate outside-the-ghetto neighbors but will actually allow him, as an adult, to beat them at their own game.

Just as the Negro athlete wins respect worldwide for his accomplishments, so can the impoverished child, who certainly knows the value of a penny, excell in life and in the business world. With the proper training and attitude-conditioning, which the Harrison System provides in abundance, almost any child anywhere can fight his way upward in adult society. The defeatist attitude seen everywhere in America can be educated out of our youth if we stop using the socialistic conventional methods employed in most elementary schools.

For the hard-pressed taxpayer, perhaps the greatest single contribution offered by the Harrison System is its ability to launch all these long-needed educational innovations for less expense. Despite our long-conditioned thinking to the contrary, the pupil-teacher ratio can rise along with achievement levels. This fact has been proven not only by me, using the system, but also by another educator of another century and country.

In London, England, over two hundred years ago, there arose a school teacher who declared that he could successfully teach more than two hundred students at one time. He did just that by utilizing pupil assistance, and then he established a number of schools where his pupils progressed far beyond anything his contemporaries could accomplish. But, as usual with something daringly new, public apathy took over and this innovative educator's accomplishments eventually died in an atmosphere of public ignorance. Today, anyone has to dig deep even to discover the name of that wonderful man.

Actually the concept of ever smaller classes is very detrimental to the cherished American virtue of self-reliance. When pupils have instant adult assistance available, there is little need and no inclination to demonstrate much individual initiative. Not realizing this fact, the uninformed and misinformed public insists on patronizing only those private schools advertising the smallest class size. And even worse, any rise in the teacher-pupil ratio of any school brings out dissenting parents like nothing else will do. Perhaps with only conventional methods available, the cry for smaller classes may seem justifiable. But I hope, by now my reader knows of something better.

There are a few noteworthy educators who believe as I do and have cried out in the wilderness. Probably their efforts have also met with the same solid ambition of administrative empire-builders as mine did. I shall reveal only one of the more daring and outspoken.

Professor Arthur Pearl, while at a college in Oregon, made the following statements in an article entitled *"Are You Sure Pupils are Better Off At School?"* published in the August 1966 issue of *Nation's Schools*:

> If we reduce class size, education will be better. If we give teachers time to prepare for classes, they will do better. If we improve pupil personnel services and pour in psychologists and social workers, we can overcome children's handicaps. We know these things—or do we?
>
> There is no evidence to support this "knowledge." And if we researched it, I would predict that very little of the above would pay off one iota over an extended period of time.
>
> Available data make it clear that none of these things by themselves produce better education. In fact, we have increasing evidence that nothing positive takes place in the classroom.

Dr. Pearl cites the case of Omar Milton to support his contention that class size has little effect on learning.

> Omar Milton, professor of psychology at the University of Tennessee, is considered to be an effective teacher. He is dynamic, interesting, well liked by his students.
>
> One semester, he ordered a random half of his students not to show up in class. These students took the midterm and the final, and at the end of the semester, he found the half that didn't show up at class did better than the half that did. Two years later, they were still doing better. They were more interested in psychology; they had a higher grade point average; fewer had dropped from school. On every possible objective and subjective index, they were doing better for not having been in class. This experiment has been repeated in many places with the same finding. I am sure that we would find it true in secondary schools if it were tested. If we ordered kids to stay home, they'd be better off. In Milton's experiment, despite the fact that teacher-pupil ratio was down because half the students were home, there was no gain for those attending class.

As it is in any industry or business anywhere, only a *better product* with more production can drive the cost of education down to a level where the taxpayer can afford it. The Harrison System's built-in incentive plan, with pupil assistance, can't fail to achieve the desired results. Perhaps I can explain in more detail how the system can accomplish this almost unbelievable miracle:

First it must be apparent by now that I do not have twenty-five or thirty children dragging their educational feet—motivation in my room is very high. With the student-teacher system, each slow student has individual help, and I am informed immediately of any academic or discipline problem. This advantage accrues whether I have twenty or sixty pupils in the class.

In addition, each pupil gets almost the same individual instruction no matter how many students are in the room since my class is broken down into groups of six. As an example, with a class of thirty I have *five* student teachers who have five pupils each. A class of sixty has *ten* teachers also with five pupils each. For practical purposes I have increased the students that I must instruct individually only by five, since my student teachers are qualified to pass onward any information I may teach.

At this point I would have my reader pause a moment to consider what such a suggested change could mean in terms of dollars and cents. For the master teachers who could competently instruct sixty pupils, salaries might double overnight. Instead of $8,000 annually, such a teacher might expect to receive $16,000 with no increased cost to the school district or lowering of educational standards and values. Besides the possibility of much greater monetary benefits, the Harrison System carries many other advantages for the classroom teacher. More than 13 years of use, revision, and careful investigation, can substantiate the following advantages:

Academic Advantages:

A. Advance can be doubled, or more, in all academic subjects, due to self-motivation.

B. Homework assignments are not necessary—pupils willingly do extra credit work at home.

C. Academic basics are easy and fun to learn—the teacher has more fun teaching them.

D. No letter grades (except at report card time), gives more flexible, yet, accurate marking.

E. Meaningful motivation for all children too young to appreciate future rewards.

F. Instant aid for the academically slow.

G. Leadership training for the academically talented.

H. Less laborsome motivation preparations are necessary, thus faster learning and more free time for the teacher.

I. Less clerical work for teacher, hence more instruction time possible.

J. All-day learning takes place in most subjects, therefore, more retention.

K. Creativity is more easily achieved.

L. No special capabilities, talents, or training, beyond those possessed by every conventional teacher, are necessary to use the Harrison System.

M. There is less nervous tension due to the absence of the motivation pressure customarily required from parents and teacher. However, minimums are set with instant help available to reach them. Also, instruction is given in emotional control leading to a happy adulthood.

N. Student self-discipline causes discipline problems to disappear.

O. Cheating is never a problem since unearned and stolen "dollars" reduce the buying power of others (usually friends).

P. There is less dependency upon the teacher's personal idiosyncrasies.

Social Advantages:

1. The student learns that anything may be obtained by earning it.

2. The pupil further learns that not only is work rewarding, but that laziness brings a just and merited punishment if carried beyond an acceptable minimum.

3. Pupils act more mature and self-reliant (the classroom is composed of doers rather than passive watchers and listeners).

4. Students are more socially adjusted and know how to emotionally handle competition.

5. Respect for law and order is learned through experience. (Infractions of rules bring a fine and one student may sue another for damage.)

6. The race relations problem is solved (by group experiences) through the understanding and respect of each other's strengths and weaknesses.

7. Our economic way of life is learned through never-to-be-forgotten experiences. (This pupil spends and saves wisely or suffers the unpleasantness of bankruptcy.)

8. Actual business experiences aid in understanding out capitalistic society.

9. Students understand by experience the advantages of democracy and freedom vs. the evils of communism and dictatorship.

10. The purchased pleasure trips introduce new areas of leisure time interest, thereby reducing the chances of children returning to pseudo-pleasures such as drugs and alcohol.

11. Partial or full inauguration of the system may be effected and developed in accordance with the individual personality and needs to the teacher (Any part of the system may be instituted or withdrawn at any time).

12. In summation, children will have training they truly can understand and retain in living the kind of life they may expect to meet as an adult.

In conclusion, perhaps I can offer a few worthwhile pieces of advice to any instructor who wishes to implement the system. This chapter is titled "What the System Can Do for You," but I wouldn't want it to do for you what it did for me. Therefore, my first caution must be to heed an age-old maxim in human relationships: If you want to do business with a man never anger him first. Perhaps, in the beginning, if I had approached my top administrators with the system on a partnership basis, they might have been willing to become involved in its development. Seldom is anyone able to see fault in his own baby.

Go to your administrator and ask his permission to experiment with the system. There is a good chance he will give his blessing to your request, and if so, you're on your way. Believe it or not, even after all my frustrations, I honestly feel that most school administrators are not like mine used to be. They are interested in the welfare of the children in their charge and have come to realize what is happening to society as a result of neglect in their duties. Some principals and superintendents even take this aspect of their employment so seriously that they visit classrooms and talk with teachers and parents to gauge the success of educational programs.

Hopefully, you will be fortunate enough to have a conscientious administrator to whom you can appeal. Such a person will be perspicacious enough to see the value of what you propose and may even be eager to try the method on all of his employees.

I feel that if all educators join hands with the Harrison System we can lift education to previously undreamed heights. But before this can be accomplished the powers in charge must first clear the tracks of present inefficient practices. Margaret V. Evans, a language arts teacher at Stow (Ohio) Junior High School, provides not only a very cleverly written article but one filled with marvelous insight. This article is appropriately titled "Clear the Tracks!" and was published in the May 1967 issue of *The Clearing House:*

Mrs. Evans likens seventh grade students to passengers about to board a train. The educators, who load the train (our on-going educational system), are labeled as "pupil-pickers." These pupil-picking educators are presently promoting a terrible type of togetherness with early adolescents. They plaster labels on kids from which they never recover.

Mrs. Evans tells us that these pupil-pickers put the upper-strata children into Pullman cars where they are pushed, academically, until their ulcers show. The middle-strata kids are loaded aboard with their happy-items, such as comic books and other paraphernalia. Over in the freight yard, they are cramming the box-cars with lower-strata youngsters—the failures who scrawl four letter words on the walls and are ready for any old riot or disturbance.

Just what happens to this train? The author has stated it so eloquently that nothing less than her exact words will do:

> Those high-average Pullman riders may emerge as ultra feminine bores, their leadership potentials lost in the labels of "egghead," "brain," and "square."
>
> That overcrowded coach train with the tremendous group of average is so overwhelming in size that the whole will be lost in the depths of mediocrity. The "near-hoods" and "hoods" are already in the depths.
>
> Is this democracy that produces these assorted children?
>
> Let's adopt some classes where pupils teach pupils and let those high-average light the torch of learning for some of those less well-endowed.
>
> Let's give the average a chance! Each one of those bouncey ones has several classes in which he excels. Let's down-grade grades and up-grade pupils. Let's stop giving the "enriched" discouragingly large amounts of homework, and allow them some time for dreams. Let's have books for those in the freight cars and caboose—books that they can master, not books that master them.
>
> Let's take the child of the moment—this seventh-grader—and attempt to meet his needs as an individual. Let's do away with study halls, and substitute instruction in reading. Let's have teachers who understand this age and who will really work at teaching. Let's remember those short attention spans. Let's mix all the children together into one long Pullman.
>
> We may have a few less juvenile delinquents. We may have a few less riots.

CHAPTER 17
For Parents and PTA's

This final chapter brings me to the court of last appeal—the parent. I have come to realize that this probably should have been my first approach. For it is the parent who receives the product of what the teacher fashions and, through the Parent-Teacher's Association, the parent has the power to change education for the better.

I know now that I should have written a book detailing "home use" for the system instead of the skimpy outline and manual I produced for my system teachers and private-school parents. Effective family use of the system could motivate local classroom utilization. But until I can write and publish such material I hope parents will persuade teachers of the system's merits. Perhaps a few illustrations can be offered for this purpose.

One of my most enthusiastic supporters became deeply involved in her daughter's education and induced two teachers in her child's school to try the system. She used the following techniques as she went about the task. She persuaded her child's teacher to read the instructional manual I had written on the system. Once the teacher implemented the system, this civic minded parent offered to physically and financially help with the student earned trips (she later confessed more self-pleasure than the pupils). Once she had her system-showcase built, she introduced—with teacher and principal approval—a self-financed bonus for scholastic increases. Achievement improvement for the whole class brought a suitable reward for the teacher and individual pupils earned theirs at auction time.

Another system supporter in a nearby city became the local PTA President and proposed a unique demonstration for her members.

"I used your manual," she said, "to illustrate the possibilities of the system and then persuaded some of our local resource people to express their opinions before our entire membership. After this I opened the meeting to a lively pro and con discussion. Someone in the audience suggested a future teacher's tea for further informal discussions of possible system use, which eventually resulted in motivating three teachers to try the system."

When I asked her how she overcame the customary teacher objections, she smiled knowingly and said there had really only been one. "All our altruistic instructors were worried sick about the excessive materialistic and commercial aspects of the system," she grinned, "until I reminded them of their own recent plea to the school board for a salary raise."

Perhaps at this point some cautions should be mentioned for the overzealous. Don't expect every teacher to embrace the system or to be successful with it if they do. Diversity is what makes the world go round and keeps life as pleasant and interesting as it is. Many teachers are not physically or mentally suited for the system and vice versa.

For instance, I recall instructing a system teacher whom I shall call a socialist for want of a better word. She learned enough to proceed with her warped sense of equalization. None of her better students were allowed to earn extra credit dollars. Only the lower half of the class was paid for outside work. Soon this instructor had a revolt on her hands and the class rejected the system. Fortunately this teacher valued the success the system brought more than she did her twisted philosophical ideals. She followed my advice and her class became motivated once again.

Other prospective system instructors can't bring themselves to permit sufficient pupil participation—they have done it all themselves as perfectionists for so long that even the idea of pupil fumblings make them feel ill. Some self-seeking instructors might even try to use the system to overextend their pupils academically, despite the small likelihood of such a result if the program is operated as it should be.

Although there is some possibility of system misuse, I am convinced that time will take care of such malfunctions just as it did with the so-called socialist teacher cited earlier. As long as the overzealous parent doesn't become discouraged, it really matters little who is approached to inaugurate the system. In fact, I would now prefer a system recruit who is somewhat weak and needs the support and reorienting my program can provide. A strong, excellent instructor cannot begin to do the harm to children that his counterpart can when using contemporary methods.

To state the case boldly for any parent or PTA organization desirous of system promotion, only good can come of your efforts. Every teacher approached with system information eventually will be very grateful for all of his or her professional career. The title of this book is not mere rhetoric. Everyone is looking for a lot for a little, and teachers are no exception. Once the system is set up correctly it will provide new incentives for students and teachers alike.